KB088501

에이스 English Readings

에 이 스 English Readings

| 고창석 편저 |

도서출판 동인

머리말

오늘날 개인의 영어 읽기능력은 사회 각 분야에서 나름의 역할을 하는 데 중요한 요소로 작용한다. 달리 말하면 개인적으로 그 능력을 향상시키는 것이 분야별 리더가 되는 필요조건이라고 할 수 있다.

이 책은 학생들에게 영어읽기에 대한 관심을 증대시키고 읽기 능력을 증진시키는 데 도움을 주려는 의도에서 다양한 읽기자료들을 선택했으며 각 단원의 자료들은 어느 정도 서로 관련이 있도록 했다. 아울러 쉬운 내용의 글과 다소 어려운 내용의 글을 각 단원에 포함시켜 학생 스스로 읽기능력을 가늠하도록 구성했다.

학생들이 사전을 찾아봐야 할 단어들이라고 편찬자가 임의적으로 판단한 어휘나 어구는 각 읽기 단원 말미에 덧붙여 가급적 읽기가 중단되지 않도록 했다.

더불어 심화학습, 내용파악이나 독해에 필요한 연습문제, 문법사항 등을 추가하고 학생들이 흥미를 가질 수 있는 내용들을 선택하여 가능한 전체적으로 간결하게 구성했다.

영어능력을 향상시키기 위해서는 풍부한 어휘 및 관용어의 확보와 문장구조에 대한 이해, 그리고 끊어 읽기를 연습하는 반복적인 학습이 무엇보다 필수적이다.

이 책이 학생들의 영어읽기 향상에 도움이 되기를 기대한다.

편저자

CONTENTs

Unit 1

1-1. *Etiquette*

1-2. *Koreans' Drinking Culture*

1-3. *The Far and the Near*

1-1.
Etiquette

Etiquette is merely acting like a well-bred human being should act. However, the meaning behind some polite customs is not always apparent at first glance. The custom of saluting,[1] for example, stems from the days when knights wore armor.[2] Their helmets[3] covered their faces to such an extent that[4] it was impossible to recognize even one's best friend. Therefore it became customary for knights to identify themselves by lifting the visors[5] of their helmets. Nowadays, the average soldier does not wear a visor, but he still preserves this old medieval[6] custom by saluting.

Shaking hands is another polite custom with an old history. During the Middle Ages it was very dangerous to travel because of the large number of robbers that lurked[7] along the roads. Therefore, when two travelers met, they

---

1 saluting 거수경례
2 armor 갑옷
3 helmet[hélmit] 투구
4 to such an extent that ~(that 이하)할 정도로
5 visors (투구의) 면갑, 안면가리개
6 medieval[mi:dii:vl] 중세의
7 lurked 숨어있는, 잠복한

commonly extended their hands to show that they carried no weapons. Today the handshake is merely a sign of our good will and sincerity, but we also express our friendliness by various greetings.[8] Such expressions as "How are you?" and "I hope you're feeling well" are designed to express our interest in the welfare of others. Even the word goodbye is a shortened form of "God be with you." Such expressions stem from man's desire to be friendly and polite.

The old saying "When in Rome do as the Romans do" is never more true than[9] at the dinner table. In some parts of Korea, it is a sign of appreciation to drink one's tea or soup with much gusto[10] and smacking[11] of lips. But in most Western countries no noise should be made while eating. Eating utensils,[12] too, differ from country to country. The Korean use chopsticks, while Western people usually employ the knife and fork. Even the manner of holding a knife and fork, however, varies from country to country, and it is certainly wise to make a little preliminary[13] study of eating habits before traveling to a foreign country. This precaution[14] can save the traveler a lot of embarrassment.

Ignorance of social usage can result in many blunders.[15] A young couple of newlyweds from the country went to New York on their honeymoon. To celebrate the occasion, they decided to have dinner at a fashionable restaurant. The dinner proceeded without incident until almost the end when the waiter placed two small silver bowls of warm water before the bride and groom. To

---

8 greetings 인사
9 to be nevermore true (important) than when ~때처럼 느낄 때는 없다.
10 with much gusto 아주 입맛을 다시며
11 smacking 쩍쩍 입맛을 다심
12 utensils 도구
13 preliminary 예비의, 임시의, 사전의
14 precaution 조심, 경계, 예방책
15 can result in many blunders 많은 실수를 저지를 수 있다. cf. Too much ambition often results in a man's downfall. Not dressing warmly in winter can result in catching a bad cold.

the girl's horror, her husband picked up the dish and began to drink the water. Her face turned scarlet[16] as she fervently[17] hoped that no one had noticed that her husband drank the water in his finger bowl.[18] Later this incident became a family joke, but at the time it was no laughing matter.

Pattern Usage

1. to be customary to: ~가 보통이다, ~가 습성이 되다.
   It is customary to remove your shoes before entering a Korean house.
   In many countries it is customary to give flowers to people who are sick.

2. to result in: ... 때문에 ~이 되다.
   Mr Kim's complaints about the dinner resulted in a fight with his wife.

3. promptly: 곧(immediately)
   When John entered the room, everyone promptly stopped talking.

16 scarlet 주홍색
17 fervently 열심히
18 finger bowl 손 씻는 그릇

Exercise

A. What does *shrug one's shoulders* mean?

a. It is a movement of the body. It means "I don't know."

b. It is an answer to a question. It means "I'll tell you later."

c. It is an action. It answers a question about directions.

d. It is a gesture. It means "I don't like you."

B. Which words in each of the following sentences give clues to the meanings of the underlined words? Circle the words. Then circle the letter of the word or words that give the correct meaning of the underlined vocabulary item.

1. The wind outside was very loud: thus when he spoke, he had to shout.

a. speak loudly b. sing c. explain the situation

2. He looked worried. His hands were shaking, and he was biting his lip.

a. relaxed b. nervous c. hungry

C. Choose the closest meaning to the underlined.

1. The custom of saluting, for example, stems from the days when knights wore armor.

a. stands out b. comes from c. bursts out d. results from

2. Eating utensils, too, differ from country to country.

a. vary from country to country

b. specialize country to country

c. characterize country to country

d. identify country to country

1-2.

Koreans' Drinking Culture

—Bernard Rowan[1]

Korea's drinking culture isn't "bottom's up." That's vulgar. Also, drinking until one spews[2] isn't it; that's a nonsense. Let's remember that conversation and company make the drink taste better.

A recent article in a British newspaper cited statistics that Koreans "drink fast to get drunk" and consume many shots of liquor weekly.[3] TIME magazine even reported Koreans the world's hardest drinkers.

Try Korea's spirituous liquors with others as part of a meal. There is the etiquette of Korea's drinking culture. There are suitable gestures to display, including holding one's arm at the elbow or the cup with both hands to show respect. After the senior pours, a junior fills his glass.

It's also usual that a friend, old or new, will present his glass to you. You drink his glass because he admits or likes you.

---

1 *The Korea Times*, 2014, may 14. The writer is assistant provost for curriculum and assessment, professor of political science and faculty athletics representative at Chicago State University.

2 spews: vomits

3 http://www.dailymail.co.uk/news/article-2551059/South-Koreans-drink-TWICE-Russians-five-times-Brits.html

Korea makes so many good drinks. Dongdongju is like makgeolli but more viscous.[4] Drink it cold, usually in bowls. It's wonderful accompaniment to food. There are a great many Korean drinks made from rice including Andong soju, a refined drink.

There are countless regional drinks, flower and fruit wines, and liquors viewed as having medicinal properties. Korean regional liquors come in various boxes with glasses and other ornaments.[5]

The Korean drinking culture shows charm, variety and a sense of fun. Koreans also enjoy many foreign types of liquor, including cognac and Scotch.

Another powerful combination is poktanju. Americans call it a boiler-maker. I recommend a different drink called osipseju, which combines baekseju (100-year wine, which mixes various herbs with rice wine) and soju. It's best served in a nice teapot at some Korean restaurants.

Professors can drink with students. It's supposed to be respectful and helps break down barriers between the learned and learners. This drinking context shows Korea's equality. We must pass the torch of life to the next generation.

Korean people leave work to go eat and drink. Then they go back to work. I don't think Korea's economic miracle could have occurred with Korea's drinking culture. Energy builds with morale[6] and collegiality.[7]

Go to a noraebang and sing with your friends while enjoying Korean drinks and side dishes. It's a great way to spend the evening, even if the singing often begs another drink rather than applause. However, we must all realize that sharing glasses and communal drinking exposes us to risk. On the other

4 [viskəs] 끈적이는, 점성이 있는
5 ornaments: decorations
6 [mouræl] 사기, 근로의욕
7 collegiality 동료 간의 협조

hand, it's like the chalice at a Catholic Mass.[8] We have no other way but to believe in others.

Hangovers[9] and drunken acts seem notorious, but hepatitis and cirrhosis[10] can follow long and heavy drinking exposure. Drinking heavily brings on mortality. You'll see people stumbling, leaning, careening[11] in subways. I advise you to hire a driver after enjoying "a few too many."[12] Better yet, learn to uphold your limits regardless. In the past it was rare to see women enjoying alcohol in public at all. Women served drinks rather than enjoyed company in drinking.

But it is pleased that drinking with friends isn't something just for men nowadays. Women should enjoy a drink too. After all, Korea's drinking culture remains part of your advanced culture.

---

8 it's like the chalice at a Catholic Mass 가톨릭 미사에서 사용하는 성배와 비슷하다.

9 hangover 숙취

10 hepatitis and cirrhosis 간염과 경변 cf. hepat(o)- '간장'을 뜻하는 결합사(모음 앞에서는 hepat-)

11 careen 기울어지다

12 have a few too many 거나하게 마시다

1-3.

The Far and the Near

— Thomas Wolfe[1]

On the outskirts of a little town upon a rise of land that swept back from the railway there was a tidy little cottage of white boards, trimmed vividly with green blinds. To one side of the house there was a garden neatly patterned with plots of growing vegetables, and an arbor[2] for the grapes which ripened late in August. Before the house there were three mighty oaks which sheltered it in their clean and massive shade in summer, and to the other side there was a border of gay flowers. The whole place had an air of tidiness, thrift, and

1 Thomas Clayton Wolfe (1900–1938) was a major American novelist of the early 20th century. Wolfe wrote four lengthy novels, plus many short stories, dramatic works and novellas. He is known for mixing highly original, poetic, rhapsodic, and impressionistic prose with autobiographical writing. His books, written and published from the 1920s to the 1940s, vividly reflect on American culture and mores of the period, albeit filtered through Wolfe's sensitive, sophisticated and hyper-analytical perspective. He became very famous during his own lifetime.
After Wolfe's death, his chief contemporary William Faulkner said that Wolfe may have had the best talent of their generation. Wolfe's influence extends to the writings of famous Beat writer Jack Kerouac, authors Ray Bradbury and Philip Roth, among others. He remains one of the most important writers in modern American literature, as he was one of the first masters of autobiographical fiction. He is considered North Carolina's most famous writer. (From Wikipedia)

2 arbor (덩굴 등을 얹은) 정자

modest comfort.

Every day, a few minutes after two o'clock in the afternoon, the limited express between two cities passed this spot. At that moment the great train, having halted for a breathing-space at the town near by, was beginning to lengthen evenly into its stroke,[3] but it had not yet reached the full drive of its terrific speed. It swung into view deliberately, swept past with a powerful swaying motion of the engine, a low smooth rumble of its heavy cars upon pressed steel, and then it vanished in the cut. For a moment the progress of the engine could be marked by heavy bellowing[4] puffs of smoke that burst at spaced intervals above the edges of the meadow grass, and finally nothing could be heard but the solid clacking tempo of the wheels receding into the drowsy stillness of the afternoon.

Every day for more than twenty years, as the train had approached this house, the engineer had blown on the whistle, and every day, as soon as she heard this signal, a woman had appeared on the back porch of the little house and waved to him. At first she had a small child clinging to her skirts, and now this child had grown to full womanhood, and every day she, too, came with her mother to the porch and waved.

The engineer had grown old and gray in service. He had driven his great train, loaded with its weight of lives, across the land ten thousand times. His own children had grown up and married, and four times he had seen before him on the tracks the ghastly[5] dot of tragedy converging like a cannon ball to its eclipse of horror[6] at the boiler head—a light spring wagon filled with

---

3 stroke 전후 왕복운동

4 heavy bellowing 크게 울림

5 ghastly: horrible

6 converging like a cannon ball to its eclipse of horror 대포 탄환처럼 공포의 엄폐물에 집중하는

children, with its clustered row of small stunned faces; a cheap automobile stalled upon the tracks, set with the wooden figures of people paralyzed with fear; a battered hobo[7] walking by the rail, too deaf and old to hear the whistle's warning; and a form flung with past his window with a scream—all this the man had seen and known. He had known all the grief, the joy, the peril and the labor such a man could know; he had grown seamed[8] and weathered in his loyal service, and now, schooled by the qualities of faith and courage and humbleness that attended his labor, he had grown old, and had the grandeur and the wisdom these men have.

But no matter what peril or tragedy he had known, the vision of the little house and the women waving to him with a brave free motion of the arm had become fixed in the mind of the engineer as something beautiful and enduring, something beyond all change and ruin, and something that would always be the same, no matter what mishap,[9] grief or error might break the iron schedule of his days.

The sight of the little house and of these two women gave him the most extraordinary happiness he had ever known. He had seen them in a thousand lights, a hundred weathers. he had seen them through the harsh bare light of wintry gray across the brown and frosted stubble of the earth,[10] and he had seen them again in the green luring sorcery of April.

He felt for them and for the little house in which they lived such tenderness as a man might feel for his own children, and at length the picture of their lives was carved so sharply in his heart that he felt that he knew their

7 a battered hobo 지친 뜨내기 일꾼
8 grown seamed 주름살이 깊어지다
9 mishap: misery
10 stubble[stʌbəl] of the earth 그루터기만 남은 밭

lives completely, to every hour and moment of the day, and he resolved that one day, when his years of service should be ended, he would go and find these people and speak at last with them whose lives had been so wrought[11] into his own.

That day came. At last the engineer stepped from a train onto the station platform of the town where these two women lived. His years upon the rail had ended. He was a pensioned servant of his company, with no more work to do. The engineer walked slowly through the station and out into the streets of the town. Everything was as strange to him as if he had never seen this town before. As he walked on, his sense of bewilderment and confusion grew. Could this be the town he had passed ten thousand times? Were these the same houses he had seen so often from the high windows of his cab? It was all as unfamiliar, as disquieting as a city in a dream, and the perplexity of his spirit increased as he went on.

Presently the houses thinned into the straggling outposts of the town,[12] and the street faded into a country road—the one on which the women lived. And the man plodded on[13] slowly in the heat and dust. At length he stood before the house he sought. He knew at once that he had found the proper place. He saw the lordly oaks[14] before the house, the flower beds, the garden and the arbor,[15] and farther off, the glint[16] of rails.

Yes, this was the house he sought, the place he had passed so many times, the destination he had longed for with such happiness. But now that he had

---

11 wrought[rɔːt] (古・文語) work의 과거・과거분사
12 the straggling ~ town 도시 외곽에 흩어져 사는 사람들의 거주지
13 plod on(trudge on) 터벅터벅 걷다
14 the lordly oaks 당당한 참나무
15 arbor 수목
16 glint: flash

found it, now that he was here, why did his hand falter[17] on the gate; why had the town, the road, the earth, the very entrance to this place he loved turned unfamiliar as the landscape of some ugly dreams? Why did he now feel this sense of confusion, doubt, and hopelessness?

At length he entered by the gate, walked slowly up the path and in a moment more had mounted three short steps that led up to the porch, and was knocking at the door. Presently he heard steps in the hall, the door was opened, and a woman stood facing him.

And instantly, with a sense of bitter loss and grief, he was sorry he had come. He knew at once that the woman who stood there looking at him with a mistrustful eye was the same woman who had waved to him so many thousand times. But her face was harsh and pinched and meager;[18] the flesh sagged wearily in sallow folds,[19] and the small eyes peered at him with timid suspicion and uneasy doubt. All the brave freedom, the warmth and the affection that he had read into her gesture, vanished in the moment that he saw her and heard her unfriendly tongue.

And now his own voice sounded unreal and ghastly[20] to him as he tried to explain his presence, to tell her who he was and the reason he had come. But he faltered on, fighting stubbornly against the horror of regret, confusion, disbelief that surged up in his spirit, drowning all his former joy and making his act of hope and tenderness seem shameful to him.

At length the woman invited him almost unwillingly into the house, and called her daughter in a harsh shrill voice. Then, for a brief agony of time, the

---

17 falter: hesitate

18 harsh and pinched and meager 거칠어지고 쇠잔하고 말라졌다

19 the flesh sagged wearily in sallow folds 피로에 지친 누르께하게 접힌 푹 가라앉은 살집

20 ghastly: horrible

man sat in an ugly little parlor, and he tried to talk while the two women stared at him with a dull, bewildered hostility, a sullen, timorous restraint.[21]

And finally, stammering a crude farewell, he departed. He walked away down the path and then along the road toward town, and suddenly he knew that he was an old man. His heart, which had been brave and confident when it looked along the familiar vista of the rails, was now sick with doubt and horror as it saw the strange and unsuspected visage of an earth which had always been within a stone's throw of him,[22] and which he had never seen or known. And he knew that all the magic of that bright lost way, the vista of that shining line, the imagined corner of that small good universe of hope's desire, was gone forever, could never be got back again.

–From *Understanding Fiction*

21 a sullen, timorous restraint 부루퉁하고 소심한 자제심

22 as it saw ~ within a stone's throw of him 언제나 자신의 지척에 있던 땅의 모습이 이상하고 생각지도 않은 모습으로 보였을 때

Exercise

1. Imagine a person's unstable mind when he is retired from his work.

2. Also, discuss the occasions when you feel isolated, alienated, or lonely from your family, friends, or acquaintances.

3. What does the short story's title, "The Far and the Near" imply?

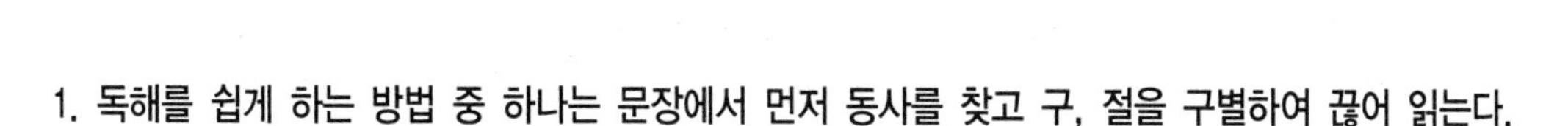

Reading Tips

1. 독해를 쉽게 하는 방법 중 하나는 문장에서 먼저 동사를 찾고 구, 절을 구별하여 끊어 읽는다.

ex) Max Weber believes that/ "man is an animal/ suspended in webs of significance/ he himself has spun."[23]

끊어 읽기를 습관화함으로써 내용을 정확하고 빠르게 파악할 수 있다.

(1) Slow readers usually read one word at a time.

ex) People/ express/ their/ personalities/ in/ their/ clothes,/ their/ cars,/ and/ their/ homes. (X)

(2) Average readers usually read a few words together (short phrases) at a time.

ex) People express/ their personalities/ in their clothes,/ their cars,/ and their homes. (△)

(3) Fast readers usually read several words (longer phrases) at a time.

ex) People express their personalities/ in their clothes, cars, and homes. (O)

2. 글의 맥락을 파악하고 어휘는 글과 관련시켜 그 의미를 이해한다.

ex) [American] people everywhere were buying folding tray-tables so they could eat their TV Dinners while glued to the box. America was well on its way to becoming a nation of *couch potatoes*, though that expression would not, of course, be used for many years.[24]

여기서 box는 TV set(수상기)를 말하며, 텔레비전에서 광고하는 식품들을 소비하며 텔레비전을 시청하고, 소파에 앉아 감자 칩을 먹으며 텔레비전 시청하는데 많은

---

23 Clifford Geertz, *The Interpretation of Cultures* (London: Hutchinson), 1975, p. 5.
24 Bryson, *Made in America*, p. 230 참조.

시간을 보내는 사람을 뜻하는 속어가 나왔다.

3. 단락(paragraph)마다 key word와 key sentence를 찾는다.

ex) In 1882, domestic **electricity** at last became a possibility on a commercial basis. By mid-decade, two hundred of New York City's wealthiest households were enjoying the illumination of five thousand light bulbs—or *electric lamps*, as the Edison company called them. Only the very wealthiest could afford such an indulgence. A single bulb cost a dollar—half a day's earnings for the average working person—and cost up to twenty cents an hour to run.[25]

4. 이해가 쉽게 되지 않거나 의문스러운 부분을 노트하고 그에 대해 질문내용을 만들고 해결한다.

ex) Many people got their first glimpse of television at the New York World's Fair in 1939. *The New York Times*, with what was threatening to become a customary lack of prescience[26], forecast that it would never be a serious competitor for radio because "people must sit and keep their eyes glued on a screen; the average American family hasn't time for it."[27]

(1) 뉴욕타임즈 신문이 텔레비전과 라디오를 비교한 예견에서 텔레비전이 실패할 것으로 본 이유는 무엇인가?

(2) glimpse, television, eyes의 단어들의 공통점은?

(3) prescience, forecast와 비슷한 단어들을 독서카드에 정리해 본다.

5. 구두법(Punctuation)

Punctuation often provides clues to the meaning of sentences and paragraphs. Italics (이탤릭체 a slanted kind of print) sometimes emphasize words.

---

25 Bryson p. 224 재인용.

26 prescience 예지, 선견(foresight), 통찰

27 Bryson p. 229 참조.

A meaning or an explanation is sometimes in parentheses (괄호), after a dash (–), or after a comma (,). Sometimes the meaning is in another sentence or sentence part.

ex) Most women work because the family needs money, not because they need more freedom. (*Money* is the important word in the sentence because it is in contrast to *freedom*.)

ex) Mexican *tacos* (meat and vegetables in *tortillas*–a flat kind of Mexican bread) are popular in the southwestern part of the United States. People eat them with *hot sauce*, a sauce of tomatoes and spicy chili peppers.
What are tortillas? They are a flat kind of Mexican bread. What are tacos? They are tortillas with meat and vegetables in them. What is hot sauce? It is a sauce of tomatoes and spicy chili peppers.

6. Quotation marks(인용부호) can introduce a new word or indicate a special use of a word or expression.

ex) Wives usually have to "pay" for the benefits of freedom and power. (The word *pay* usually refers to money. It has a different meaning in this sentence.)

7. 연결사(transition words)

Transition words (*in other words*, *that*, *also*, *in addition*, *however*, and so on) often provide clues to the meaning of sentences and paragraphs. The following words and expressions have similar meanings: Like the connecting word so, they all show an effect.

〈therefore, consequently, because of this, thus, as a result, for this reason〉

ex) There were beautiful beaches and facilities for water sports; *thus*, it was a perfect place for a vacation. (Because there were beautiful beaches and facilities for water sports, it was a perfect place for a vacation.)

In the past, grandparents, parents, and children used to live together. *In addition*, sometimes brothers with their families were part of this extended family. (In other words, grandparents, parents, children, brothers, and brothers' families all lived together.)

Women have more freedom in the nuclear family. This freedom, *however*, can be a disadvantage. (Because freedom is usually an advantage, the idea of a "disadvantage" is not expected. The second sentence presents a contrast to the first.)[28]

* **독해를 향상시키기 위해서는 우선 내용이 자신에게 흥미로운 책을 선택한다. 지나치게 특정 분야에 전문적이거나 어려운 내용을 선택하지 않도록 한다. 비교적 짧은 단편이나 중편의 글을 골라 하루나 일주일 안에 독파하고 중요 내용과 그와 관련한 생각들을 노트하도록 한다. 예를 들어 권장할만한 영어 연설문, 수필, 단편 등은 다음과 같다.**

Abraham Lincoln, "Gettysburg Address"
Martin Luther King, "I Have a Dream"
James Joyce, "Araby"
George Orwell, *Animal Farm*
Ernest Hemingway, "Indian Camp," *The Old Man and the Sea*
Edith Hamilton, *Mythology* 또는 *Bulfinch's Mythology: The Age of Fable*

28 Elaine Kirn et al, *Interactions I: A Reading Skills Book* (New York: McGraw-Hill Publishing Co.) p. 63, 78, 31.

Unit 2

2-1. *The Energy of Life*

2-2. *Self-esteem*

2-3. *On the Meaning of Life*

2-1.

The Energy of Life

All life depends on energy. To grasp this truth, it is necessary to go back to the beginning of what we call 'life.' We already know enough to conclude that the conditions on other planets in our solar system will not give us a study of life making that compares with the Earth's history.

The Earth is about 4.5 billion years old. About 3 billion years ago its crust[1] became relatively stable. There seems to be general agreement that the atmosphere was lacking in free oxygen, but that there were such gases as methane, water vapor,[2] ammonia, hydrogen, carbon dioxide,[3] carbon monoxide, and nitrogen[4]—elemental groupings that could react with each other. In the laboratory these gases of the primeval[5] atmosphere have been energized by electrical discharges[6] and by ultraviolet rays, and the derivatives[7] have been

---

1 crust 껍질, 외피, 지각(地殼)

2 water vapor 수증기

3 carbon dioxide 이산화탄소. di는 그리스어로 2를 뜻하고 oxide는 산화물(부록 1을 참조).

4 nitrogen 질소

5 primeval: prehistoric, primitive

6 discharge 방전(放電)

7 derivative 파생물

identified as amino acids and other organic molecules[8] necessary for the process called 'life.' The vigorous[9] reaction of these gases to ultraviolet light is important because, since there was no free oxygen in the original atmosphere, the ultraviolet radiations from the sun were not modified[10] by ozone (O_3) and were therefore much stronger. Most of this chemistry probably took place in the upper atmosphere,[11] and the molecules were precipitated[12] by rain and collected in the seas, where they reacted upon one another. They formed aggregations[13] that, in turn,[14] became more complex. Some were more efficient than others in attracting elements out of the environment (like later creatures competing for food) and so grew at the expense of[15] the less efficient. This was a primitive beginning for natural selection.[16]

Meanwhile, changes were taking place in the atmosphere. Hydrogen, the lightest gas, escaped rapidly. By the time of 2 billion years ago, organic synthesis[17] had taken place and the organic process had become self-sustaining.[18]

---

8 molecule 분자
9 vigorous 활기찬
10 modify 완화, 조절하다
11 upper atmosphere 초고층 대기
12 precipitated 응결되다
13 aggregations 집합(체)
14 in turn 번갈아, 차례차례
15 at the expense of ~의 비용으로, ~을 희생하여
16 natural selection 자연도태
17 synthesis 합성
18 self-sustaining 개체유지. sustain 지탱, 유지, 지속하다 (n) sustenance 지지, 유지, 지속
cf. sustainability 지속가능성

2-2.

Self-esteem

During the past ten years, scientists at Weslyan University in Connecticut, and at the University of California have been measuring the self-esteem of young boys, the respect that they have for themselves.

The boys were given many tests. Their personality was measured, their feelings and thoughts about people and life were examined. As the boys grew older, they were studied in school, at work, and how they acted socially.

At first, the boys were asked to write down just what they thought of themselves as people; and what they thought they might be able to do with their lives. This test examined how well the boys were able to measure their own abilities and talents.

Then, each boy was given a special test which measured his abilities. What the boys wrote and what the tests showed were then carefully studied.

From these groups of boys were tested further. Their memory, understanding, hopes and behavior in all situations were measured. From these tests, the scientists were able to draw a good picture of the self-esteem of those tested.

Boys with high self-esteem were found to active and easily able to say what they thought. They were successful in school and in their relations with people. In discussions, they led rather than listened. They were always ready to express their thoughts and ideas. They were not troubled by criticism. They were highly interested in world problems.

As children, the high self-esteem boys were creative, not destructive. They believed in themselves and in their abilities. They were sure they could do whatever they started.

They were happy to meet other persons, knowing that they would be well received. They had few physical problems. They did not easily become tired. They did not suffer from headaches or stomach disorders.

In many ways, the group of boys with middle self-esteem were like the higher self-esteem group. They also talked and expressed their ideas freely. They saw the world as a happy and good place. They too were not troubled with criticized.

These boys in the middle group, however, were not sure of their own value as people. They did their best work when they knew other people liked them.

The boys with low self-esteem were different from the other two groups. These boys were sad most of the time. They seemed not to have the courage to start things going. They felt alone and unloved. They could not say what was on their minds. They could not defend themselves very well. Anger frightened them, and they took special care not to make others angry. In a group discussion or at school, they remained in the shadows, listening, not talking.

Exercise

* Discuss the followings.

Their bellies flat with lack of feasting. The trail is long and they travel fast. (Life)

"It is well. I am as a last year's leaf, clinging lightly to the stem. My eyes no longer show me the way of my feet, and my feet are heavy, and I am tired. It is well." (Irony)

Nature was not kindly to the flesh. She had no concern for that concrete thing called the individual. To life she set one task, gave one law. To perpetuate was the task of life, its law was death.

* 다음 문장에서 서로 관련 있는 말을 찾아 쓰시오.

There was the time of the Great Famine, when the old men crouched empty-bellied to the fire. (clue: stomach)

The chief was his son, stalwart and strong, head man of the tribesmen, and a mighty hunter. (clue: manly)

* Choose the closest one to the underlined.

1. For long he <u>pondered</u> on the days of his youth.
   a. lamented b. deplored c. thought d. regretted

2. As the women <u>toiled</u> with the camp luggage, his voice rose chiding them for their slowness.
   a. blamed b. scolded c. punished d. labored

2-3.

On the Meaning of Life

—H. L. Mencken[1]

You ask me, in brief, what satisfaction I get out of life, and why I go on working. I go on working for the same reason that a hen goes on laying eggs. There is in every living creature an obscure[2] but powerful impulse to active functioning.[3] Life demands to be lived. Inaction, save as a measure of recuperation between bursts of activity,[4] is painful and dangerous to the healthy organism—in fact, it is almost impossible. Only the dying can be really idle.

The precise form of an individual's activity is determined, of course, by the equipment[5] with which he came into the world. In other words, it is determined by his heredity.[6] I do not lay eggs, as a hen does, because I was born without any equipment for it. For the same reason I do not get myself elected to

---

1 Henry Louis Mencken (1880-1956) 미국 작가이자 비평가. 1933년 작성한 이 글은 The Story of Philosophy의 저자인 Will Durant가 Mencken에게 인생의 의미가 무엇인지 설명해 달라고 부탁한 편지에 대해 답한 것이다.

2 obscure: unclear

3 powerful impulse to active functioning 활동적인 기능을 수행하고자 하는 강한 충동

4 save as a measure of recuperation between bursts of activity 강렬한 활동 중에 회복하는 수단으로는 제외하고

5 equipment 자질(資質)

6 heredity 유전

Congress, or play the violoncello[7], or teach metaphysics[8] in a college, or work in a steel mill. What I do is simply what lies easiest to my hand. It happens that I was born with an intense and insatiable[9] interest in ideas, and thus like to play with them. It happens also that I was born with rather more than the average facility for putting them into words. In consequence, I am a writer and editor, which to say, a dealer in them and concocter[10] of them.

There is very little conscious volition[11] in all this. What I do was ordained[12] by the inscrutable[13] fates, not chosen by me. In my boyhood, yielding to a powerful but still subordinate[14] interest in exact facts, I wanted to be a chemist, and at the same time my poor father tried to make me a business man. At other times, like any other relatively poor man, I have longed to make a lot of money by some easy swindle.[15] But I became a writer all the same,[16] and shall remain one until the end of the chapter,[17] just as a cow goes on giving milk all her life, even though what appears to be her self-interest urges her to give gin.

I am far luckier than most men, for I have been able since boyhood to make a good living doing precisely what I have wanted to do—what I would have done for nothing,[18] and very gladly, if there had been no reward for it.

---

7 violoncello: cello
8 metaphysics 형이상학(the branch of philosophy that deals with the nature of reality and knowledge)
9 intense and insatiable[inséiʃəbəl] 강렬하고 물리지 않는
10 concocter 조합하는 사람
11 volition 의지력, 결단력, 의욕
12 ordained 정하다, 임명하다
13 inscrutable: mysterious, unknown
14 subordinate 부수되는, 종속적인
15 swindle 사취, 사기, 협잡
16 all the same 아무래도, 그래도
17 until the end of the chapter 최후까지, 마지막까지
18 for nothing: without reward, without reason

Not many men, I believe, are so fortunate. Millions of them have to make their livings at tasks which really do not interest them. As for me, I have had an extraordinarily pleasant life, despite the fact that I have had the usual share of woes.[19] For in the midst of those woes I still enjoyed the immense satisfaction which goes with free activity. I have done, in the main, exactly what I wanted to do. Its possible effects upon other people have interested me very little. I have not written and published to please other people, but to satisfy myself, just as a cow gives milk, not to profit the dairyman, but to satisfy herself. I like to think that most of my ideas have been sound ones, but I really don't care. The world may take them or leave them. I have had my fun hatching them.

Next to agreeable work as a means of attaining happiness I put what Huxley called the domestic affections—the day-to-day intercourse with family and friends.[20] My home has seen bitter sorrow, but it has never seen any serious disputes, and it has never seen poverty. I was completely happy with my mother and sister, and I am completely happy with my wife. Most of the men I commonly associate with are friends of very old standing.[21] I have known some of them for more than thirty years. I seldom see anyone, intimately, whom I have known for less than ten years.[22] These friends delight me. I turn to them when work is done with unfailing eagerness.[23] We have the same general tastes, and see the world much alike. Most of them are interested in music, as I am. It has given me more pleasure in this life than any other

---

19 woe[wou] 1. 비애, 고뇌 cf. grief, sorrow 2. (보통 복수) 재난

20 Next to agreeable work ~ and friends. 행복을 성취하는 방법으로서 하고 싶은 일을 하는 것 다음으로 나는 헉슬리가 가정적 애정이라고 일컬었던 가족들, 친구들과의 일상적인 교제다. cf. put B next to A: B를 A 다음에 두다. (중요성이나 비중 따위에 있어서) A 다음으로 B이다.

21 standing: duration

22 I seldom see ~ for less than ten years. 가깝게 교우관계를 맺은 10년 이하의 사람은 거의 없다.

23 when work is done with unfailing eagerness 일을 열정을 가지고 잘 마쳤을 때

external thing. I love it more every year.

As for religion, I am quite devoid of[24] it. Never in my adult life have I experienced anything that could be plausibly called a religious impulse. My father and grandfather were agnostics[25] before me, and though I was sent to Sunday-school as a boy and exposed to the Christian theology I was never taught to believe it. My father thought that I should learn what it was, but it apparently never occurred to him that I would accept it. He was a good psychologist. What I got in Sunday-school—besides a wide acquaintance with Christian hymnology[26]—was simply a firm conviction that the Christian faith was full of palpable absurdities,[27] and the Christian God preposterous.[28] Since that time I have read a great deal in theology—perhaps much more than the average clergyman—but I have never discovered any reason to change my mind.

The act of worship, as carried on by Christians, seems to me to be debasing[29] rather than ennobling. It involves grovelling[30] before Being who, if He really exists, deserves to be denounced[31] instead of respected. I see little evidence in this world of the so-called goodness of God. On the contrary, it seems to me that, on the strength of[32] His daily acts, He must be set down[33] as a most stupid, cruel, and villainous[34] fellow. I can say this with a clear

24 quite devoid of ~이 전혀 없는
25 agnostics 불가지론자들
26 hymnology 찬송가
27 palpable absurdities 명백한 부조리들
28 preposterous: God (was) preposterous (ridiculous, foolish).
29 debase 저하시키다, 떨어뜨리다.
30 grovelling 엎드림
31 deserves to be denounced 마땅히 비난받아야 할
32 on the strength of~: relying on~, influenced by~
33 set down: considered, regarded, thought, viewed
34 villainous[vilənəs] fellow 악랄한 자

conscience, for He has treated me very well—in fact, with vast politeness. But I can't help thinking of His barbaric torture of most of the rest of humanity. I simply can't imagine revering[35] the God of war and politics, theology and cancer.

I do not believe in immortality, and have no desire for it. The belief in it issues from the puerile[36] egos of inferior men. In its Christian form it is little more than a device for getting revenge upon those who are having a better time on this earth. What the meaning of human life may be I don't know: I incline to suspect that it has none. All I know about it is that, to me at least, it is very amusing while it lasts. Even its troubles, indeed, can be amusing. Moreover, they tend to foster the human qualities that I admire most—courage and its analogues.[37] The noblest man, I think, is that one who fights God, and triumphs over Him. I have had little of this to do. When I die I shall be content to vanish into nothingness. No show, however good, could conceivably be good forever.

35 revere[riviər] 존경하다, 숭배하다.
36 puerile: boyish; of little importance
37 analogues 동류어(同類語)들

Grammatical Tips

● It의 용례

(1) 지시대명사

ex) Misfortune will never leave me till I leave it.

(2) 가주어, 가목적어

ex) It takes great wisdom to laugh at one's own misfortunes.

(3) 비인칭 주어(날씨, 거리, 명암, 등을 표현 할 때)

ex) It never rains but it pours. 불행은 겹친다.
It was very lonely. 무척 쓸쓸했다.

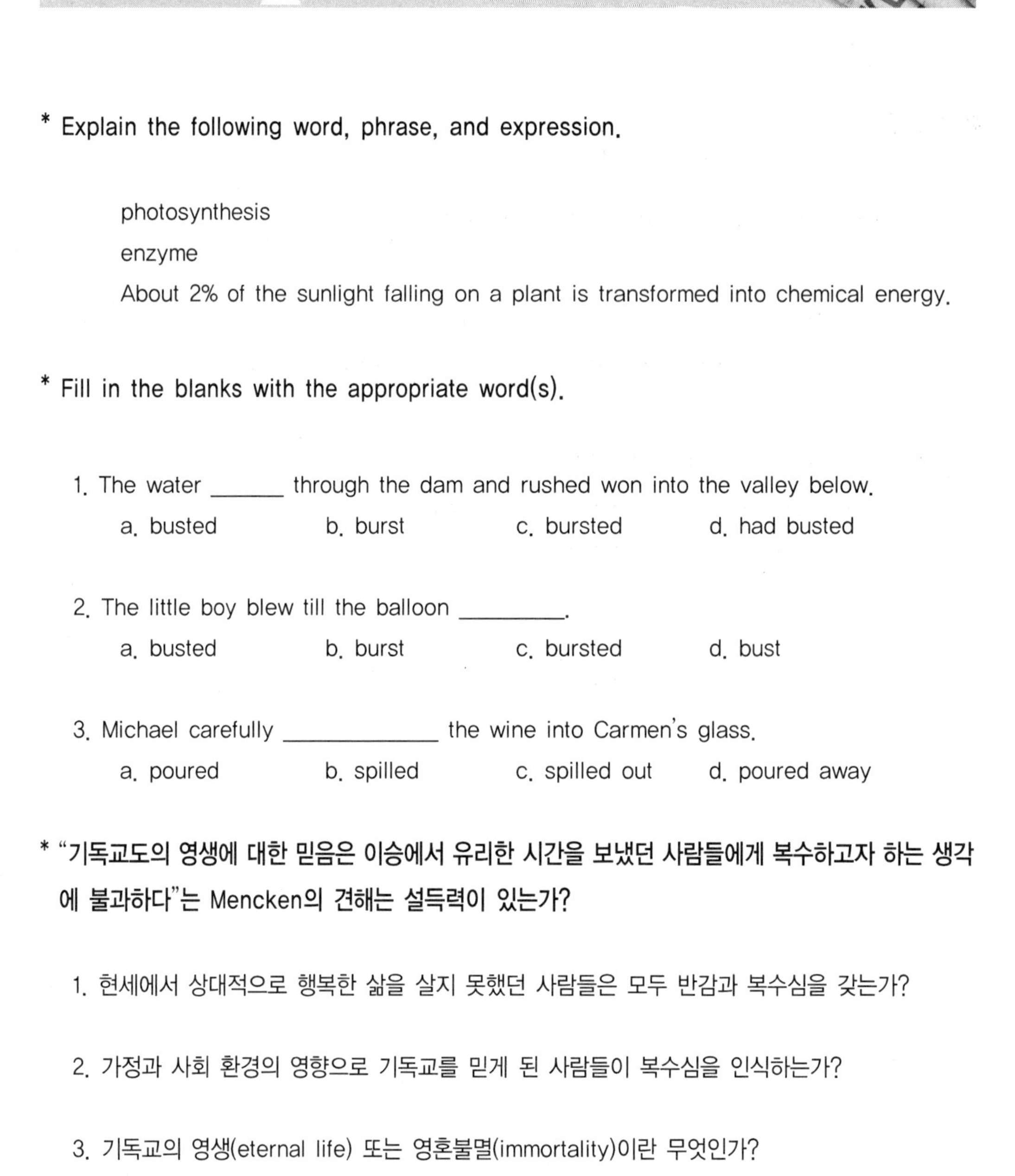

Exercise

* Explain the following word, phrase, and expression.

photosynthesis

enzyme

About 2% of the sunlight falling on a plant is transformed into chemical energy.

* Fill in the blanks with the appropriate word(s).

1. The water ______ through the dam and rushed won into the valley below.
   a. busted b. burst c. bursted d. had busted

2. The little boy blew till the balloon ________.
   a. busted b. burst c. bursted d. bust

3. Michael carefully ____________ the wine into Carmen's glass.
   a. poured b. spilled c. spilled out d. poured away

* "기독교도의 영생에 대한 믿음은 이승에서 유리한 시간을 보냈던 사람들에게 복수하고자 하는 생각에 불과하다"는 Mencken의 견해는 설득력이 있는가?

1. 현세에서 상대적으로 행복한 삶을 살지 못했던 사람들은 모두 반감과 복수심을 갖는가?

2. 가정과 사회 환경의 영향으로 기독교를 믿게 된 사람들이 복수심을 인식하는가?

3. 기독교의 영생(eternal life) 또는 영혼불멸(immortality)이란 무엇인가?

Unit 3

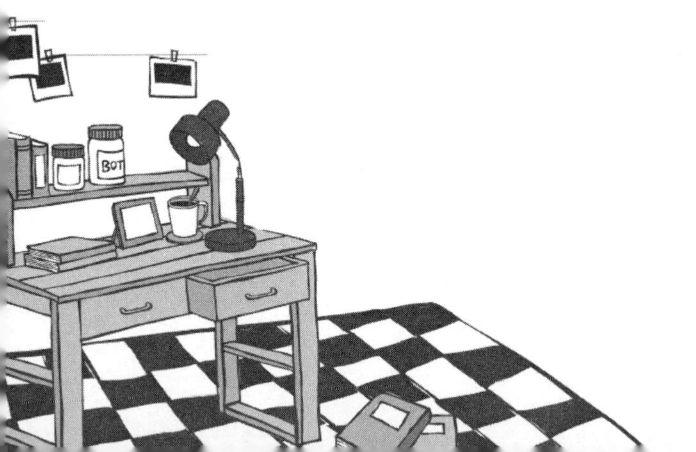

3-1.

Word Power and Knowledge

All normal human beings are born with a powerful urge to learn. Almost all of them lose this urge,[1] even before they have reached maturity.[2] It is only the few who are so constituted[3] that lack of learning becomes a nuisance.[4] This perhaps the most insidious[5] of human tragedies.

Children are wonders at increasing their vocabularies because of their "powerful urge to learn." They do not learn solely by means of words, but as their knowledge increases, so does their vocabulary—for words are the symbols of ideas and understanding.

If you are a parent, you perhaps remember that crucial and trying[6] period in which your child constantly asked "Why?" The "Why?" is the child's method of finding out. How many adults that you know go about[7] asking and thinking

---

1 urge 충동
2 maturity: adult
3 constitute 구성하다
4 nuisance 성가심, 귀찮음
5 insidious: harmful
6 crucial and trying: important and hard (trying experience 쓰라린 경험)
7 go about 꾸준히 ~하다

"Why?" How often do you yourself do it?

The adults who "lose this urge," who no longer feel that "lack of learning becomes a nuisance" stop building their vocabularies. They stop learning, they stop growing intellectually, they stop developing mentally, they stop changing.

But fortunately the process is not irreversible.[8]

We have not yet learned to bring back life to a dead body. But we do know how to breathe life into a stalled[9] mind, how to revive[10] intellectual curiosity, and how to restore[11] the "powerful urge to learn."

In short, we do know how to help an adult start his vocabulary growing again even if it has been quiescent[12] for many years. You may think that after you pass the twenties you rapidly and inevitably lose your ability to learn. That is simply not true. There is no doubt that the years up to eighteen or twenty are the best period for learning. Your own experience bears that out.[13] And of course with the average person more learning is done up to twenty than ever after. That is why one's vocabulary increases so spectacularly[14] for the first twenty years of one's life and comparatively little thereafter.

The fact that most learning is accomplished before the age of twenty does not mean that very little learning can be done beyond that age. Although the learning curve rises spectacularly up to twenty, it remains steady for at least another five years. After that, ability to learn drops very slowly up to the age of thirty-five, a little more rapidly but still slowly beyond that age. Right up to

8 irreversible 돌이킬 수 없는
9 stalled 향상하지 못하고 정체된
10 revive 소생시키다
11 restore 회복하다
12 quiescent[kwaiesənt] 정지된; 조용한
13 bear a person or a thing out 확증하다, 뒷받침하다(conform, support)
14 spectacularly 눈에 띄게

senility[15] the total decrease in learning ability after twenty is never more than 15 per cent. No matter what your age, you can go on learning efficiently, or start learning once again if perhaps you have stopped.

Words are the symbols of knowledge, the keys to accurate thinking. Is it any wonder then that the most successful and intelligent people have the biggest vocabularies? It was not their large vocabularies that made these people successful and intelligent, but their knowledge. Knowledge, however, is gained largely through words. In the process of increasing their knowledge, these successful people increased their vocabularies. Knowledge is chiefly in the form of words, and from now on, you will be thinking about, and thinking with, new words and new ideas.

15 senility[siniləti] 노년, 노쇠(기)

Grammatical Tips

● 형용사 어미(Adjective Suffixes) –ful, –less

You can use the suffixes *–ful* and *–less* to make adjectives from some nouns. The suffix *–ful* often means "with" or "full of." The suffix *–less* often means "without." For example, the word *careful* means "full of care" and *careless* means "without care."

–able: avail (v. 소용에 닿다), –ic, –ical (astrology 점성학), –al (recreation 휴양, 레크리에이션, nation, profession), –y (lengthy), –ive (successive), 명사+ly (friendly, worldly), –ing (causing a feeling), –ed (having a feeling)

● 접미사: –ology (the study of; the science of), –er, –ist (a person who), –scope (an instrument something for seeing)

● 접두사: The prefix (beginning) of a word often gives a clue to its meaning. Some prefixes give negative meanings to words; they create words with opposite meanings.

ex) The *discontented* expression on his face told me that he was *unhappy*.
(***Dis****contented* is the opposite of *contented*; ***un****happy* is the opposite of *happy*.)

The following prefixes mean "no" or "not": un–, in–, im–, dis–, il–, ir–, re–(again), trans–(across), tele–(far)

Exercise

* Change each of the following words to its opposite meaning by using one of preceding prefixes.

married, natural, possible, equal, healthful, known, satisfied, pelasant, advantage, similar, fortunate, appear, honest, polite

* Complete the chart by making adjectives from the nouns. Notice which nouns take only one of the suffixes. Pay attention to spelling with *beauty*; you will have to change *y* to *I*.

Noun	Adjective with *-ful*	Adjective with *-less*
care	careful	careless
use		
beauty		x
hope		
harm		
price	x	
help		
wonder		x
thought		
pain		
health		

A. Complete each sentence with the appropriate adjective from the chart above.

1. Don't be ________ when you drive. You could have an accident.

2. The operation was _________. I didn't feel a thing. (cf. ache)

3. This is such a _______ tool. I use it all the time.

4. Scientists are __________ they will find new medicines in nature.

5. I'm sorry, I wasn't thinking. It was _________ of me not to offer to help.

6. It was the best party I've ever been to. It was __________!

7. This antique necklace is _________. No amount of money could ever replace it.

8. The researchers were disappointed when they found that the new substance was ____________ against disease.

B. In each of the following sections, fill in the blank with the correct form–noun, verb, or adjective. Choose from the words above each section.

〈competition, competitor, compete, competitive〉

1. Vegetarians ar not usually __________ people.

2. Students often have to ______ for grades.

3. McDonald's and Burger King are ________s in the fast–food business; they are in __________ with each other.

〈management, manager, manage, manageable〉

4. Her major at the university is business __________.

5. Who is going to _________ the new health–food store?

6. A man from the Midwest is going to be the new __________.

7. I'm afraid this is not a ________ problem.

⟨forgetfulness, forget, forgetful⟩

8. Why do I always _________ new vocabulary items?

9. I am a very _________ person.

10. _________ is a big problem for me.

3-2.

Food Preservation

Long ago people had no way to keep food from spoiling. So they ate all they possibly could and hoped it wouldn't be too long before the next meal. Mealtime was any time they found food, so they were either stuffed[1] or starved most of the time.

No one knows for sure how people first learned to preserve food. Maybe they accidentally left food in the sun and discovered that the dried food kept longer. Maybe they left food by the fire and found out that cooked food not only kept longer, but tasted better. Somehow someone learned that salt helps preserve meat and fish and even vegetables. For example, pickles are cucumber that are preserved with salt. Through the years, people have continued to learn new and better ways of preserving food from one growing season to another. And totally millions of people work in jobs that have something to do with food preservation.

Suppose you were walking up and down the aisles of a modern supermarket. On the shelves you would find food preserved in many different

1 stuffed: filled up by eating too much

ways. You would see canned tomatoes and peaches in glass jars. These foods were first sealed in airtight[2] containers and then heated to a high temperature. If there was a break in the seal, the food would soon spoil. You would also see dried and powdered foods on the shelves. You would see prunes (which are dried plums) and raisins (which are dried grapes). You would see powdered milk and powdered eggs. Some dried foods, such as onions and potatoes, can be kept almost indefinitely.

If you walked past the dairy counter, you would find many foods that have been treated to kill any harmful germs that might have been in them. Milk is a good example. Raw milk—that is, milk just as it comes from the cow—may be unsafe to drink. If the milk is heated and then cooled, the harmful germs are killed. The man who discovered this way of treating milk was a Frenchman by the name of Louis Pasteur.[3] Milk so treated is called pasteurized[4] milk and the process is called pasteurization.

In the supermarket you would also find many frozen foods—frozen fruits, vegetables, meat, and fish. As techniques for freezing food are being improved, more and more frozen foods are appearing on the market, and more and more people are buying them. Fruits and vegetables sold in the supermarket are often frozen as soon as they are picked. The sooner fruits and vegetables are frozen, the better. Freezing machines can be taken into the fields where the food grows, so that little time is lost between picking and freezing.

Many Americans with large families now have their own freezers and freeze their own food. Because fruits and vegetables are cheaper when they are

---

2 airtight: too tight for air or gas to enter or escape 밀폐된
3 Pasteur (1822–1895), French chemist and bacteriologist
4 pasteurize: heat and suddenly cool milk or other things to destroy harmful bacteria

in season[5] the housewife often buys more than she can use in a few days or even in a week and then freezes the rest. Preparing food for the freezer is a fairly simple process. To prepare strawberries, for example, the housewife simply needs to clean them. Put them on a tray in the freezer for a few hours, and then put them in plastic bags. Bread, cakes, and pies (cooked or uncooked) can also be kept in a freezer.

With the improvement in methods of food preservation, people no longer have to stuff one day and starve another. They can have a well-balanced diet year round.

5 in season: available fresh for use as food

Exercise

* Read the following selection quickly. Then answer the questions.

Human Diet

What does the typical North Americans usually eat? Most people think that the typical North American diet consists of fast foods—hamburgers and French fries. It also includes convenience foods, usually frozen or canned, "junk food" without much food value—candy, potato chips, cereal with lots of sugar but no vitamins—and so on. This diet is very high in sugar, salt, fat, and cholesterol, and the choice of food does not provide much good nutrition.

However, eating habits are changing. North Americans are becoming more interested in good health, and nutrition is an important part of health. People are eating less red meat and fewer eggs, and they are eating more chicken and fish. They know that chicken and fish are better for their health than meat or eggs because these foods do not contain much fat or cholesterol. Some foods might cause health problems, and people want to stay away from them.

For health reasons, many people are also buying more fresh vegetables. They may eat them without cooking them first, or they might cook them quickly in very little water because they want to keep the vitamins.

The "typical" North American diet now includes food from many different countries. More ethnic restaurants are opening in big cities in the United States and Canada. Foods from Japan, Thailand, Mexico, West Africa, China, and

Indonesia are very popular. At lunchtime, many people go to ethnic fast-food places for a Mexican taco, Middle Eastern falafel,[6] or Philippine lumpia.[7]

How are we going to eat in the future? We will probably continue to eat more fish and vegetables and less meat. We will still buy convenience foods, but frozen foods will be better for our health, and canned foods will have less salt and sugar. Our "junk food" in the future is not really going to be "junk" at all, because instead of candy bars we are going to eat "nutrition bars" with a lot of vitamins and protein. In the future, our diet will probably be even more interesting and healthful than it is now.[8]

A. Write the meanings of the underlined words in the following sentences.

1. Most people think that the typical North American diet consists of fast foods (hamburgers and French fries). It also includes convenience foods, usually frozen or canned, and "junk food"—candy, potato chips, cereal with lots of sugar but no vitamins, and so on.

fast foods:
convenience foods:
junk food:

---

6 falafel[fəlaːfəl] 야채 샌드위치

7 Lumpia are pastries of Chinese origin similar to fresh popiah or fried spring rolls popular in Southeast Asia. The term lumpia derives from Hokkien lunpia (Chinese: 潤餅), which is an alternate term for popiah. The recipes, both fried and fresh versions, were brought by Chinese immigrants from the Fujian province of China to Southeast Asia and became popular where they settled in Indonesia and the Philippines.

8 Elaine Kirn et al, *Interactions I: A Reading Skills Book* (New York: McGraw-Hill Publishing Co.) p. 30.

2. People are eating more chicken and fish—foods without much fat or <u>cholesterol</u> (a kind of fat).

cholesterol:

3. The "typical" North American diet now includes food from many different countries—"<u>ethnic</u>" foods.

ethnic:

4. The typical American <u>diet</u> includes convenience foods and junk food without much food value. This choice of food is very high in sugar, salt, and fat, but it does not provide much good <u>nutrition</u>.

diet:
nutrition:

5. For health reasons, many people are also buying more <u>raw</u> vegetables. They may eat the vegetables uncooked, or they might cook them quickly in very little water.

raw:

B. Circle the number of the one main idea of the reading.

1. The "typical" North American diet now includes food from many different countries.
2. For health reasons, many people are also buying more raw vegetables.
3. Our "junk food" in the future is not really going to be "junk" at all.
4. North Americans are becoming more interested in good health, and nutrition is an important part of health.

C. Match the following words on the left-hand side with their meanings on the right-hand side. Write the correct letter on the line.

1. ___ calories	a. an artificial ingredient
2. ___ serving	b. things in food
3. ___ gram	c. not natural
4. ___ artificial	d. units of food energy
5. ___ label	e. elements of food in things like rice, bread, and potatoes
6. ___ minerals	f. average amount of a kind of food for one person for one meal
7. ___ ingredients	g. the necessary daily amount of a food element for one person
8. ___ carbohydrates	h. natural element in food, such as copper or zinc
9. ___ additive	i. a unit of weight
	j. the paper on a food package with nutritional information

3-3.

Memory and Aging

One of the key concerns of older adults is the experience of memory loss, especially as it is one of the hallmark[1] symptoms of Alzheimer's disease. However, memory loss is qualitatively different in normal aging from the kind of memory loss associated with a diagnosis of Alzheimer's. Occasional lapses[2] in memory are normal in aging adults and understanding the distinction between normal symptoms and warning signs of Alzheimer's is critical in maintaining cognitive health.

Memory Decline in Normal Aging

Normal aging is associated with a decline in various memory abilities in many cognitive tasks. Studies comparing the effects of aging on episodic memory, semantic memory, short-term memory and priming[3] find that episodic memory is especially impaired in normal aging; some types of short-term

---

1 hallmark 특징
2 lapses 경과, 흐름; 착오, 실수; 쇠퇴
3 priming 정보를 얻기 cf. prime(v)은 (발화)준비하다, 마중물을 붓다, 정보를 얻다

memory are also impaired. The deficits[4] may be related to impairments seen in the ability to refresh recently processed information.

Source information[5] is one type of episodic memory that suffers with old age; this kind of knowledge includes where and when the person learned the information. Knowing the source and context of information can be extremely important in daily decision-making, so this is one way in which memory decline can affect the lives of the elderly. Therefore, reliance on political stereotypes[6] is one way to use their knowledge about the sources when making judgments, and the use of meta-cognitive[7] knowledge gains importance. This deficit may be related to declines in the ability to bind information together in memory during encoding and retrieve[8] those associations at a later time.

Prevention and Treatment

The use of memory aids is helpful in fighting cognitive signs of aging. Keeping a "to do" list will help assure that certain tasks are completed and not forgotten. Establishing day-to-day routines will make everyday tasks, such as taking medication, easier to remember if they occur at the same time every day. Putting everything in its rightful place will help to avoid confusion. Keeping important items in a place where they can always be seen will save you time when they're needed. Using simple associations to remember names, events, or objects can make recalling things much easier. Finally, keeping a calendar to display important dates and times will make remembering much easier.

---

4 deficits 부족, 결손 (반) surplus
5 source information 근원(원천) 정보
6 stereotypes 고정관념
7 metacognitive 초인식적인
8 retrieve 만회(회복)하다

The easiest way to prevent memory decline in elderhood is to stay active throughout your 40's and 50's. Being mentally active and learning new skills during middle adulthood and as you age is speculated to lower the risk of Alzheimer's disease. By performing new tasks and learning new skills, the brain is forced to focus more than it would on a task in which you have already mastered. In essence, acquiring new skills is a way to exercise your brain.

A 2011 study suggests that increasing Vitamin C and Vitamin E in diets can increase verbal memory functions. Vitamin C is an antioxidant that can protect brain tissues from inflammation[9] and oxidation damage. Foods rich in Vitamin C include broccoli, Brussels sprouts, cabbage, cantaloupe, cauliflower, grapefruit, green and red peppers, kale, kiwi, mango, oranges, papaya, pineapple, strawberries, and tomato juice. Vitamin E can protect brain cell membranes.[10] Foods rich in Vitamin E include almonds, canola oil, grape seed oil, hazelnuts, papaya, sunflower seeds, and wheat germ oil. Vitamin E is also prevalent in leafy greens, including beet greens, kale, mustard greens, spinach. There are conflicting opinions as to whether such vitamins must be consumed in foods or if dietary supplements are also effective.

— From Wikipedia

9 inflammation 발화, 연소
10 membranes 막, 얇은 막

Further Studies

Motivation[11] is a psychological feature that induces an organism to act towards a desired goal and elicits, controls, and sustains certain goal-directed behaviors. It can be considered a driving force; a psychological one that compels or reinforces an action toward a desired goal. For example, hunger is a motivation that elicits[12] a desire to eat. Motivation is the purpose or psychological cause of an action.[13]

Motivation has been shown to have roots in physiological, behavioral, cognitive,[14] and social areas. Motivation may be rooted in a basic impulse[15] to optimize[16] well-being, minimize physical pain and maximize pleasure. It can also originate from specific physical needs such as eating, sleeping or resting, and sex.

"Motivation is an inner drive to behave or act in a certain manner. 'It's the difference between waking up before dawn to pound the pavement and lazing around the house all day.' These inner conditions such as wishes, desires and goals, activate to move in a particular direction in behavior."[17]

Motive is a reason for action which urges a person to act in a certain

---

11 motivation 자극, 동기부여
12 elicit 이끌다
13 Schacter, Daniel (2011). *PSYCHOLOGY.* United States of America: Catherine Woods. p. 325
14 cognitive 인식의
15 impulse 충동
16 optimize 최적화하다
17 http://www.psychologytoday.com/basics/motivation

way: *Jealousy was the motive for the murder in Othello written by William Shakespeare. What do you think his motive were in helping us? We had begun to suspect his motives. I think his wife was the motive force behind his resignation.*

Motif is a main subject, pattern, idea, etc., on which a work of art is based, or from which it is developed. Or it is a single or repeated pattern or color *a cat motif on the child's pajamas.* Also, it is an often-repeated arrangement of noted in a musical work.

Exercise

A.

(a) She had two step-sisters. Their names were Drizella and Anastasia. The step-sisters never had to work. They just prance[18] around the house in their fancy dresses. And they always (b) made fun of her because her dress was so plain.

One day a letter came to the house.

"Drizella! Anastacia!" cried the stepmother.

"Listen to this!"

She (c) [red] the letter. It said:

"The King is giving a (d) ball tonight. His son, the Prince, will choose a wife. Every girl in the kingdom must be there."

1. Who is she?
   a. Anastacia b. Drizella c. Stepmother d. Cinderella

2. Make a sentence using the (b) idiom.

3. Write the proper verb referring to the phonetic symbol.

4. What does the underlined (d) mean?
   a. round object that is hit or thrown or kicked in game
   b. an object with a spherical shape
   c. the people assembled at a lavish formal dance

---

18 prance 함부로 돌아다니다.

B.

The colonists were well acquainted with a New World food that abounded[19] along the eastern seaboard:[20] the turkey. A not unreasonable question is how a native American bird came to be named for a country four thousand miles away. The answer is that when turkeys first appeared in England, some eighty years before the *Mayflower* set sail, they were mistakenly supposed to have come from Turkey. They had in fact come from Spain, brought back from Mexico by Hernán Cortés's expedition of 1519. Many other European nations made a similar geographical error in naming the bird. The French thought they came from India and thus called them *poulets d'Inde*, from which comes the modern French *dindon* (Bryson 183).

1. Why did the English people call a native American bird turkey?

2. Explain the implication of the *Mayflower* briefly, referring to the following passage.

The ***Mayflower*** was the ship that transported mostly English Puritans and Separatists, collectively known today as the Pilgrims, from Plymouth England to the New World. There were 102 passengers and the crew is estimated to be approximately 30 but the exact number is unknown. This voyage has become an iconic story in some of the earliest annals of American history, with its story of death and of survival in the harsh New World winter environment. The culmination of the voyage in the signing of the Mayflower Compact is an event which established a rudimentary form of democracy, with each member contributing to the welfare of the community.

* A great book never leaves the reader the same as he was before—he is always a better man for having read it. —André Maurois[21]

19 abounded 많은, 풍부한
20 seaboard 해안, 연안지방
21 André Maurois (1885-1967), a French author

Pronunciation Tips

● **주의해야 할 발음**

1. th 발음은 혀끝을 입 밖으로 내밀어 발음한다. 성대의 울림에 따라 다음과 같이 구별한다.
2. 무성음[θ]: think, thought, path
3. 유성음[ð] mother, the, this, that, those
4. f(ph), v는 윗니로 아랫입술을 물며 발음한다.

● **묵음(silent sound)**

1. n앞의 k: knee, knives, know
2. calm, half, comb, dumb, sword[sɔːrd],
3. pneumonia(폐렴), psychology
4. r앞의 w: write, wreath, wrap

Unit 4

4-1.

Stoicism

> "Philosophy does not promise to secure anything external for man, otherwise it would be admitting something that lies beyond its proper subject-matter. For as the material of the carpenter is wood, and that of statuary[1] bronze, so the subject-matter of the art of living is each person's own life." —Epictetus[2]

Stoicism[3] is a school of Hellenistic philosophy founded in Athens by Zeno of Citium in the early 3rd century BC. The Stoics taught that destructive emotions resulted from errors in judgment, and that a sage, or person of "moral and intellectual perfection," would not suffer such emotions.[4]

Stoics were concerned with the active relationship between cosmic determinism and human freedom, and the belief that it is virtuous to maintain a will (called *prohairesis*) that is in accord with nature. Because of this, the Stoics presented their philosophy as a way of life, and they thought that the

1 statuary 조각, 조상(彫像)

2 Epictetus, *Discourses* 1.15.2, Robin Hard revised translation.

3 stoicism 극기주의

4 *Stanford Encyclopedia of Philosophy.*

best indication of an individual's philosophy was not what a person said but how they behaved.[5]

Later Stoics, such as Seneca and Epictetus, emphasized that because "virtue is sufficient for happiness," a sage was immune[6] to misfortune. This belief is similar to the meaning of the phrase "stoic calm," though the phrase does not include the "radical ethical" Stoic views that only a sage can be considered truly free, and that all moral corruptions are equally vicious.

From its founding, Stoic doctrine was popular with a following in Greece and throughout the Roman Empire—including the Emperor Marcus Aurelius—until the closing of all philosophy schools in AD 529 by order of the Emperor Justinian I, who perceived their pagan character as being at odds with[7] the Christian faith.[8]

Basic Tenets (Doctrines)

The Stoics provided a unified account of the world, consisting of formal logic, non-dualistic physics and naturalistic ethics. Of these, they emphasized ethics as the main focus of human knowledge, though their logical theories were of more interest for later philosophers.

Stoicism teaches the development of self-control and fortitude[9] as a means of overcoming destructive emotions; the philosophy holds that becoming a clear and unbiased[10] thinker allows one to understand the universal reason (logos). A

---

5 John Sellars. *Stoicism*, p. 32.
6 immune 면한, 면역성의
7 be at odds with ~과 갈등을 일으키다.
8 David, Sedley. "Ancient philosophy." In E. Craig. *Routledge Encyclopedia of Philosophy*.
9 fortitude 용기, 인내 with fortitude 의연하게, 결연히
10 unbiased 선입관이 없는, 공평한 unprejudiced

primary aspect of Stoicism involves improving the individual's ethical and moral well-being: "*Virtue* consists in a *will* that is in agreement with Nature."[11] This principle also applies to the realm of interpersonal relationships; "to be free from anger, envy, and jealousy,"[12] and to accept even slaves as "equals of other men, because all men alike are products of nature."[13]

The Stoic ethic espouses[14] a deterministic perspective; in regard to those who lack Stoic virtue, Cleanthes once opined[15] that the wicked man is "like a dog tied to a cart, and compelled to go wherever it goes."[16] A Stoic of virtue, by contrast, would amend his will to suit the world and remain, in the words of Epictetus, "sick and yet happy, in peril and yet happy, dying and yet happy, in exile and happy, in disgrace and happy," thus positing a "completely autonomous" individual will, and at the same time a universe that is "a rigidly deterministic single whole." This viewpoint was later described as "Classical Pantheism" (and was adopted by Dutch philosopher Baruch Spinoza).[17]

Stoicism became the foremost popular philosophy among the educated elite in the Hellenistic world and the Roman Empire,[18] to the point where, in the words of Gilbert Murray "nearly all the successors of Alexander [...] professed themselves Stoics."[19]

---

11 Russell, Bertrand. *A History of Western Philosophy*, p. 254

12 앞 책 p. 264

13 앞 책 p. 253

14 espouse 신봉하다, 지지하다

15 opined: thought, held

16 앞 책 p. 254

17 Charles Hartshorne and William Reese, "Philosophers Speak of God," *Humanity Books*, 1953 Ch. 4

18 Amos, H. (1982). *These Were the Greeks*. Chester Springs: Dufour Editions.

19 Gilbert Murray, *The Stoic Philosophy* (1915), p. 25. In Bertrand Russell, *A History of Western Philosophy* (1946).

History

Beginning at around 301 BC, Zeno taught philosophy at the Stoa Poikile (i.e., "the painted porch"), from which his philosophy got its name.[20] Unlike the other schools of philosophy, such as the Epicureans,[21] Zeno chose to teach his philosophy in a public space, which was a colonnade[22] overlooking the central gathering place of Athens, the Agora.

Almost 2,300 years ago, in ancient Greece, the philosopher Zeno lectured on a topic which still piques[23] the human mind, to wit:[24] "How to Live a Happy Life." Zeno would stand on a porch (the Greek word for which is stoa) and hold forth somewhat as follows: men should free themselves from intense emotion, be unmoved by both joy and sorrow, and submit without complaint to unavoidable necessity. Today, Freudians preach almost the exact opposite—let your emotions flow freely, express your love or animosity,[25] don't bottle up[26] your feelings. But in the fourth century B.C., when Zeno was expounding his credo,[27] his philosophy of control of the passions fell on receptive ears. His followers were called Stoics, after the stoa, or porch, from which the master lectured.

Zeno's ideas developed from those of the Cynics,[28] whose founding father, Antisthenes, had been a disciple of Socrates. Zeno's most influential follower was Chrysippus, who was responsible for the molding of what is now called

20 Becker, Lawrence (2003). *A History of Western Ethics*. New York: Routledge. p. 27.
21 Epicureans 에피쿠로스(Epicurus) 설(說) 신봉자들(쾌락주의)
22 colonnade 열주, 주랑
23 piques 돋구다, 끌다
24 to wit, 즉 that is, namely
25 animosity: hostility 앙심, 적의
26 bottle up 억제하다
27 expound his credo 자기의 신조를 설명하다
28 the Cynics 키니코스[견유(犬儒)]학파(Antithenes가 창시한 고대 그리스 철학의 한 학파)

Stoicism. Later Roman Stoics focused on promoting a life in harmony within the universe, over which one has no direct control.

Scholars usually divide the history of Stoicism into three phases:

* Early Stoa, from the founding of the school by Zeno to Antipater.
* Middle Stoa, including Panaetius and Posidonius.
* Late Stoa, including Musonius Rufus, Seneca, Epictetus, and Marcus Aurelius.

Modern Usage

The word "stoic" commonly refers to[29] someone indifferent to pain, pleasure, grief, or joy. The modern usage as "person who represses[30] feelings or endures patiently" was first cited in 1579 as a noun, and 1596 as an adjective.[31] In contrast to the term "Epicurean", the *Stanford Encyclopedia of Philosophy*'s entry on Stoicism notes, "the sense of the English adjective 'stoical' is not utterly misleading with regard to its philosophical origins."[32]

– Compiled from Wikipedia

29 refers to ~라고 하다

30 repress 억누르다, 억제하다

31 Harper, Douglas (November 2001). "Online Etymology Dictionary – Stoic." Retrieved 2006-09-02.

32 Baltzly, Dirk (2004. 12. 13). "Stanford Encyclopedia of Philosophy – Stoicism." Retrieved 2006-09-02.

Proverbs

싫더라도 참아야 한다.
If you don't like it, you must lump it. —American

피할 수 없는 것은 포옹하라.
What cannot be eschew'd must be embrac'd.

인내는 미덕.
Patience is a virtue.

인내는 힘보다 큰 것을 이룬다.
Patience will achieve more than force.

천재는 돌진하고, 갈팡질팡하다 지쳐버리나, 인내는 버티다 승리한다.
Genius darts, flutters, and tires; perseverance wears and wins.

Exercise

* Choose the closest meaning to the underlined.

1. The people <u>pressed</u> the king for the reform.
   a. repressed b. objected c. promised d. admitted

2. All moral corruptions are equally <u>vicious</u>.
   a. beneficial b. good c. virtuous d. wicked

3. Justinian I perceived their <u>pagan</u> character as being at odds with the Christian faith.
   a. reasonable b. heathen c. irrational d. ignoble

4. A Stoic of virtue, by contrast, would <u>amend</u> his will to suit the world.
   a. direct b. order c. reform d. coordinate

* Answer the questions.

1. Why was Stoic doctrine closed?

2. What does Stoicism teach?

4-2.

Indian Camp

—Ernest Hemingway[1]

At the lake shore there was another rowboat drawn up. The two Indians stood waiting.

Nick and his father got in the stern[2] of the boat and the Indians shoved[3] it off and one of them got in to row. Uncle George sat in the stern of the camp rowboat. The young Indian shoved the camp boat off and got in to row Uncle George.

The two boats started off in the dark. Nick heard the oarlocks[4] of the other boat quite a way ahead of them in the mist. The Indians rowed with quick choppy strokes.[5] Nick lay back with his father's arm around him. It was cold on the water. The Indian who was rowing them was working very hard, but the other boat moved further ahead in the mist all the time.

---

1 Ernest Hemingway (1898-1961) 1954년 *The Old Man and the Sea*로 노벨 문학상을 받은 미국 소설가이며 *Farewell To Arms*, *For Whom the Bell Tolls*, *The Sun Also Rises* 등의 작품이 있다.

2 stern 고물, 선미 (반) bow

3 shove 밀다, 떠밀다

4 oarlock 노받이

5 rowed with quick choppy strokes 물결을 내며 재빨리 노를 저어 갔다

"Where are we going, Dad?" Nick asked.

"Over to the Indian camp. There is an Indian lady very sick."

"Oh," said Nick.

Across the bay they found the other boat beached. Uncle George was smoking a cigar in the dark. The young Indian pulled the boat way up on the beach. Uncle George gave both the Indians cigars.

They walked up from the beach through a meadow that was soaking wet with dew, following the young Indian who carried a lantern. Then they went into the woods and followed a trail that led to the logging road that ran back into the hills. It was much lighter on the logging road as the timber was cut away on both sides. The young Indian stopped and blew out his lantern and they all walked on along the road.

They came around a bend and a dog came out barking. Ahead were the lights of the shanties[6] where the Indian bark-peelers[7] lived. More dogs rushed out at them. The two Indians sent them back to the shanties. In the shanty nearest the road there was a light in the window. An old woman stood in the doorway holding a lamp.

Inside on a wooden bunk lay a young Indian woman. She had been trying to have a baby for two days. All the old women in the camp had been helping her. The men had moved off up the road to sit in the dark and smoke out of range of the noise she made. She screamed just as Nick and the two Indians followed his father and Uncle George into the shanty. She lay in the lower bunk, very big under a quilt. Her head was turned to one side. In the upper bunk was her husband. He had cut his foot very badly with an ax three days

---

6 shanty 오두막, 판자집

7 Indian bark-peelers 나무껍질을 벗겨 살아가는 미국 인디안

before. He was smoking a pipe. The room smelled very bad.

Nick's father ordered some water to be put on the stove, and while it was heating he spoke to Nick.

"This lady is going to have a baby, Nick," he said.

"I know," said Nick.

"You don't know," said his father. "Listen to me. What she is going through is called being in labor.[8] The baby wants to be born and she wants it to be born. All her muscles are trying to get the baby born. That is what is happening when she screams."

"I see," Nick said.

Just then the woman cried out.

"Oh, Daddy, can't you give her something to make her stop screaming?" asked Nick.

"No. I haven't any anaesthetic," his father said. "But her screams are not important. I don't hear them because they are not important."

The husband in the upper bunk rolled over against the wall.

The woman in the kitchen motioned to the doctor that the water was hot. Nick's father went into the kitchen and poured about half of the water out of the big kettle into a basin. Into the water left in the kettle he put several things he unwrapped from a handkerchief.

"Those must boil," he said, and began to scrub his hands in the basin of hot water with a cake of soap he had brought from the camp. Nick watched his father's hands scrubbing each other with the soap. While his father washed his hands very carefully and thoroughly, he talked.

"You see, Nick, babies are supposed to be born head first but sometimes

---

8 being in labor 산고(産苦), 진통

they're not. When they're not they make a lot of trouble for everybody. Maybe I'll have to operate on this lady. We'll know in a little while."

When he was satisfied with his hands he went in and went to work.

"Pull back that quilt, will you, George?" he said. "I'd rather not touch it."

Later when he started to operate Uncle George and three Indian men held the woman still. She bit Uncle George on the arm and Uncle George said, "Damn squaw bitch!" and the young Indian who had rowed Uncle George over laughed at him. Nick held the basin for his father. It all took a long time.

His father picked the baby up and slapped it to make it breathe and handed it to the old woman.

"See, it's a boy, Nick," he said. "How do you like being an interne?"[9]

Nick said, "All right." He was looking away so as not to see what his father was doing.

"There. That gets it,"[10] said his father and put something into the basin.

Nick didn't look at it.

"Now," his father said, "there's some stitches[11] to put in. You can watch this or not, Nick, just as you like. I'm going to sew up the incision I made."

Nick did not watch. His curiosity had been gone for a long time.

His father finished and stood up. Uncle George and the three Indian men stood up. Nick put the basin out in the kitchen.

Uncle George looked at his arm. The young Indian smiled reminiscently.

"I'll put some peroxide[12] on that, George," the doctor said.

He bent over the Indian woman. She was quiet now and her eyes were

9 interne: intern 수련의, 인턴

10 That gets it: That is all finished.

11 stitch 꿰맴

12 peroxide 과산화수

closed. She looked very pale. She did not know what had become of the baby or anything.

"I'll be back in the morning," the doctor said, standing up. "The nurse should be here from St. Ignace by noon and she'll bring everything we need."

He was feeling exalted and talkative as football players are in the dressing room after a game.

"That's one for the medical journal,[13] George," he said. "Doing a Caesarian[14] with a jack-knife and sewing it up with nine-foot, tapered gut leaders."[15]

Uncle George was standing against wall, looking at his arm.

"Oh, you're a great man, all right," he said.

"Ought to have a look at the proud father. They're usually the worst sufferers in these little affairs,"[16] the doctor said. "I must say he took it all pretty quietly."

He pulled back the blanket from the Indian's head. His hand came away wet. He mounted on the edge of the lower bunk with the lamp in one hand and looked in. The Indian lay with his face toward the wall. His throat had been cut from ear to ear. The blood had flowed down into a pool where his body sagged the bunk. His head rested on his left arm. The open razor lay, edge up, in the blankets.

"Take Nick out of the shanty, George," the doctor said.

There was no need of that. Nick, standing in the door of the kitchen, had

---

13 That's one for the medical journal 그건 의학 저널에 실릴만한 수술이었어.

14 Doing a Caesarian 제왕절개 수술(로마의 황제 시저가 복부 절개 수술로 출생한데서 유래)

15 tapered gut leaders 끝이 가는 낚시줄

16 They're usually the worst sufferers in these little affairs 이런 일을 당해서는 (산모의 남편과 같은) 그런 사람들이 보통 가장 심란하지

a good view of the upper bunk when his father, the lamp in one hand, tipped the Indian's head back.

It was just beginning to be daylight when they walked along the logging road back toward the lake.

"I'm terribly sorry I brought you along, Nickie," said his father, all his post-operative exhilaration gone. "It was an awful mess to put you through."

"Do ladies always have such a hard time having babies?" Nick asked.

"No, that was very, very exceptional."

"Why did he kill himself, Daddy?"

"I don't know, Nick. He couldn't stand things, I guess."

"Do many men kill themselves, Daddy?"

"Not very many, Nick."

"Do many women?"

"Hardly ever."

"Don't they ever?"

"Oh, yes. They do sometimes."

"Daddy?"

"Yes."

"Where did Uncle George go?"

"He'll turn up all right."

"Is dying hard, Daddy?"

"No, I think it's pretty easy, Nick. It all depends."[17]

They were seated in the boat, Nick in the stern, his father rowing. The sun was coming up over the hills. A bass jumped, making a circle in the water. Nick trailed his hand in the water. It felt warm in the sharp chill of the

---

17 It all depends. 경우(사정)에 따라 다르다.

morning.

In the early morning on the lake sitting in the stern of the boat with his father rowing, he felt quite sure that he would never die.

Proverbs

치료될 수 없는 것은 참아라.
What cannot be cured must be endured.

인내가 없는 사람은 지혜가 없는 사람이다.
Whoever has no patience has no wisdom. —Sa'di

Exercise

* Answer the questions.

1. Nick's father said, "But her screams are not important. I don't hear them because they are not important." What does his saying imply?
   a. Platonism   b. Epicureanism   c. Stoicism   d. Modernism

2. What is the theme of the short story?
   a. Visiting a camp   b. Indian woman's being in labor
   c. Life and death   d. A boy's being an interne

3. The doctor said to his son, "<u>It</u> was an awful mess to put you through." What does <u>it</u> mean?

* Choose the closest meaning to the underlined.

1. "Why did he kill himself, Daddy?"
   "He couldn't <u>stand</u> things, I guess."
   a. erect   b. endure   c. guard   d. represent

2. "Where did Uncle George go?"
   "He'll <u>turn up</u> all right."
   a. disappear   b. hide   c. appear   d. conceal

3. "There's some <u>stitches</u> to put in. You can watch this or not."
   a. "A stitch in time saves nine."
   b. "I have to sew up the incision."

c. "I'll put some peroxide on that."

d. "How do you like being an interne?"

*** 다음 밑줄 친 부분을 우리말로 옮기시오.**

1. What she is going through is called being in <u>labor</u>.

2. <u>Doing a Caesarian</u> with a jack-knife and sewing it up with nine-foot, tapered gut leaders.

Grammatical Tips

● 명사의 복수(Noun Pluralization)

1. -s, -es: knees, fleas, houses, boxes

2. 불규칙복수: man-men, foot-feet

   *참고: 중세 복수어미 -n: 약 1620년 무렵에 복수형어미로 -n을 덧붙였다. 그 예로 knees는 kneen, flea는 flean, houses는 housen, eyes는 eyen 등이 있는데 children, brethren, oxen 등이 이 경우에 해당한다.[18]

3. 처음부터 복수명사로 쓰이는 다음과 같은 명사들의 수량을 표시하기 위해서는 a pair of, a piece of 또는 some과 같은 수식어가 필요하다.

   glasses(spectacles), overalls(작업복), shoes, pantyhose(stockings), chopsticks, scissors, police(the를 붙여 복수로 한다), shorts, sneakers, jeans, thanks(감사), binoculars, underwear, clothes, weights(역기), fireworks(불꽃놀이), news

4. 어미에 -s나 -es가 붙지 않아도 복수로 취급되는 명사

   pantyhose, police, underwear

5. 라틴어 복수명사

   cactus-cacti, phenomenon-phenomena, stadium-stadia(stadiums) 단, data는 원래 그 단수형이 datum이지만 단수, 복수 모두 data를 쓴다.

6. 복수형으로만 쓰이는 관용구

   hundreds and thousands 수백수천의, 무수히 많은, office hours 근무시간, lots and lots 많고도 많은

---

18 Bill, Bryson, *Made in America*, p. 16 참조.

● 셀 수 없는 명사(물질, 고유, 추상명사)

1. soap, milk, water, sand, furniture, money, clothes, Kim (the Kims는 김씨 부부 또는 김씨네 가족), love, truth
2. 물질명사의 계량화: a cake of soap, a piece of furniture, two cups of milk, two bowls of rice

● 명사 어미

-ity (longevity[lɔndʒévəti] 장수; 수명; 장기근속), -tion (temptation), -sion (succession), -ance (attendance), -ence (subsistence 생존; 생계), -ship (relationship, friendship)

*주의: food는 셀 수 없는 명사로 재료나 물체를 말한다. 그러나 foods는 다양한 종류의 food를 나타낸다. 그 구별을 위해서는 a lot of나 much같은 셀 수 없는 명사를 수식하는 형용사가 오면 food로 쓰고 many, various 또는 a variety of와 같은 가산명사에 붙는 수식어가 오면 foods로 쓴다.

ex) I've never seen so much food these days.

At this year's international fair, we sampled foods from all over the world. (sampled 시식했다)

Unit 5

5-1. *A Mystery Story*

5-2. *Oedipus*

5-1.

A Mystery Story

Edgar Allan Poe was a master of the mystery story. He had a peculiar[1] talent for making the reader feel as if he were actually present at the scene of the crime. Poe's appeal is not confined[2] strictly to American readers. He is popular the world over, but particularly in Japan. In fact, one Japanese writer has adopted the name Edogawa Rampo, the Japanese equivalent of Edgar Allan Poe, in honor of the famous master of mystery. In talking about mystery stories, Sherlock Homes comes to mind as the most famous detective of fiction. His exploits[3] and adventures have delighted the hearts of mystery-story fans for generations.

Many people find an enjoyable thrill in matching wits with the great detectives of fiction. We cannot all be Sherlock Holmes in real life, but within the covers of a book we can all find an opportunity to be armchair detectives.[4] Reading a good mystery story is like becoming a member of the police force for

1 peculiar 독특한
2 confined: limited
3 exploit 업적, 위업
4 armchair detective 의자에 앉은 채 탐정 기분을 느끼는 것

a while. A good mystery story gives its readers enough clues to solve the mystery for themselves. Solving the mystery before reading the explanation in the last chapter gives the reader a sense of great accomplishment. Can you figure out[5] what is going to happen in the following incident before you come to the end? If you can, you have a great future in store for you as a detective.[6]

The Black Cat – Edgar Allan Poe[7]

Tomorrow I die. Tomorrow I die, and today I want to tell the world what happened and thus perhaps free my soul from the horrible weight which lies upon it. But listen! Listen, and you shall hear how I have been destroyed.

When I was a child, I had a natural goodness of soul which led me to love animals – all kinds of animals, but especially those animals we call pets, animals which have learned to live with men and share their homes with them.

---

5 figure out 어림하다; 산정하다; 이해하다

6 have a great future in store for you as a detective 당신이 탐정가로서 대단한 장래를 비축한 것이다.

7 Edgar Allan Poe (1809–1849) was an American author, poet, editor, and literary critic, considered part of the American Romantic Movement. Best known for his tales of mystery and the macabre, Poe was one of the earliest American practitioners of the short story, and is generally considered the inventor of the detective fiction genre. He is further credited with contributing to the emerging genre of science fiction. He was the first well-known American writer to try to earn a living through writing alone, resulting in a financially difficult life and career.

Born in Boston, he was the second child of two actors. His father abandoned the family in 1810, and his mother died the following year. Thus orphaned, the child was taken in by John and Frances Allan, of Richmond, Virginia. Although they never formally adopted him, Poe was with them well into young adulthood. Tension developed later as John Allan and Edgar repeatedly clashed over debts, including those incurred by gambling, and the cost of secondary education for the young man. Poe attended the University of Virginia for one semester but left due to lack of money. Poe quarreled with Allan over the funds for his education and enlisted in the Army in 1827 under an assumed name. It was at this time his publishing career began, albeit humbly, with an anonymous collection of poems, *Tamerlane and Other Poems* (1827), credited only to "a Bostonian". With the death of Frances Allan in 1829, Poe and Allan reached a temporary rapprochement. Later failing as an officer's cadet at West Point and declaring a firm wish to be a poet and writer, Poe parted ways with John Allan.

There is something in the love of these animals which speaks directly to the heart of the man who has learned from experience how uncertain and changeable is the love of other men.

I was quite young when I married. You will understand the joy I felt to find that my wife shared with me my love for animals. Quickly she got for us several pets of the most likeable kind. We had birds, some goldfish, a fine dog, and a cat.

The cat was a beautiful animal, of unusually large size, and entirely black. I named the cat Pluto,[8] and it was the pet I liked best. I alone fed it, and it followed me all around the house. It was even with difficulty that I stopped it from following me through the streets.

Our friendship lasted, in this manner, for several years, during which, however, my own character became greatly changed. I began to drink too much wine and other strong drinks. As the days passed, I became less loving in my manner; I became quick to anger; I forgot how to smile and laugh. My wife—yes, and my pets, too, all except the cat—were made to feel the change in my character.

One night I came home quite late from the inn, where I now spent more and more time drinking. Walking with uncertain step, I made my way with effort into the house. As I entered, I saw—or thought I saw—that Pluto, the cat, was trying to stay out of my way, to avoid me. This action, by an animal which I had thought still loved me, made me angry beyond reason. My soul seemed to fly from my body. I took a small knife out of my coat and opened

8 (1) Pluto was the ruler of the underworld in classical mythology. The earlier name for the god was Hades, which became more common as the name of the underworld as a place. In ancient Greek religion and myth, Pluto represents a more positive concept of the god who presides over the afterlife. (2) 명왕성

it. Then I took the poor animal by the neck and with one quick movement I cut out one of its fear-filled eyes!

Slowly the cat got well.[9] The hole where its eye had been was not a pretty thing to look at, it is true; but the cat no longer appeared to suffer any pain. As might be expected, however, it ran from me in fear whenever I came near. Why should it not run? Yet this did not fail to anger me. I felt growing inside myself a new feeling. Who has not, a hundred times, found himself doing wrong, doing some evil thing for no other reason than because he knows he should not? Are not we humans at all times pushed, ever driven in some unknown way to break the law just because we understand it to be the law?

One day, in cold blood, I tied a strong rope around the cat's neck, and taking it down into the cellar under the house I hung[10] it from one of the wood beams above my head. I hung it there until it was dead. I hung it there with tears in my eyes, I hung it because I knew it had loved me, because I felt it had given me no reason to hurt it, because I knew that my doing so was a wrong so great, a sin so deadly that it would place my soul forever outside the reach of the love of God!

That same night, as I lay sleeping, I heard through my open window the cries of our neighbors. I jumped from my bed and found that the entire house was filled with fire. It was only with great difficulty that my wife and I escaped. And when we were out of the house, all we could do was stand and watch it burn to the ground. I thought of the cat as I watched it burn, the cat whose dead body I had left hanging in the cellar. It seemed almost that the cat had in some mysterious way caused the house to burn so that it could make me pay

9 get well 회복하다, 좋아지다
10 hang-hung-hung 걸다, 널다 cf. hang-hanged-hanged 목매달다

for my evil act, so that it could take revenge upon me.

Months went by, and I could not drive the thought of the cat out of my mind. One night I sat in the inn, drinking, as usual. In the corner I saw a dark object that I had not seen before. I went over to see what it could be. It was a cat, a cat almost exactly like Pluto. I touched it with my hand and petted it, passing my hand softly along its back. The cat rose and pushed its back against my hand.

Suddenly I realized that I wanted the cat. I offered to buy it from the innkeeper, but he claimed he had never seen the animal before. As I left the inn, it followed me, and I allowed it to do so. It soon became a pet of both my wife and myself.

The morning after I brought it home, however, I discovered that this cat, like Pluto, had only one eye. How was it possible that I had not noticed this the night before? This fact only made my wife love the cat more. But I, myself, found a feeling of dislike growing in me. My growing dislike of the animal only seemed to increase its love for me. It followed me, followed me everywhere, always. When I sat, it lay down under my chair. When I stood up, it got between my feet and nearly made me fall. Wherever I went, it was always there. At night I dreamed of it. And I began to hate that cat!

One day my wife called to me from the cellar of the old building where we were now forced to live. As I went down the stairs, the cat, following me as always, ran under my feet and nearly threw me down.

In sudden anger, I took a knife and struck wildly at the cat. Quickly my wife put out her hand and stopped my arm. This only increased my anger and, without thinking, I turned and put the knife's point deep into her heart! She fell to the floor and died without a sound.

I spent a few moments looking for the cat, but it was gone. And I had other things to do, for I knew I must do something with the body, and quickly. Suddenly I noted a place in the wall of the cellar where stones had been added to the wall to cover an old fireplace which was no longer wanted. The walls were not very strongly built, and I found I could easily take down those stones. Behind them there was, as I knew there must be, a hole just big enough to hold the body. With much effort I put the body in and carefully put the stones back in their place. I was pleased to see that it was quite impossible for anyone to know that a single stone had been moved.

Days passed. Still there was no cat. A few people came and asked about my wife; but I answered them easily. Then one day several officers of the police came. Certain that they could find nothing, I asked them in and went with them as they searched.

Finally they searched the cellar from end to end. I watched them quietly, and, as I expected, they noticed nothing. But as they started up the stairs again, I felt myself driven by some unknown inner force to let them know, to make them know, that I had won the battle.

"The walls of this building," I said, "are very strongly built; it is a fine old house." And as I spoke, I struck with my stick that very place in the wall behind which was the body of my wife. Immediately I felt a cold feeling up and down my back as we heard coming out of the wall itself a horrible cry.

For one short moment the officers stood looking at each other. Then quickly they began to pick at the stones, and in a short time they saw before them the body of my wife, black with dried blood and smelling of decay. On the body's head, its one eye filled with fire, its wide-open mouth—the color of blood, sat the cat, crying out its revenge!

Pattern Usage

* Find each idiom in the following.

1. When applying for a job, it is important to be courteous.
2. The florist seems to have quite a talent for flower arranging.
3. Sometimes, when we're trying to explain something, the proper expression just won't come to mind.
4. I thought about the puzzle for a long time, but he couldn't figure out the answer. (understand)
5. Not a few students have great difficulties figuring out what to major in at college.
6. The dentist was surprised that the man could stand so much pain. (bear, put up with)
7. If it rains tomorrow, we'll have to call the picnic off. (cancel)

Reading Comprehension

1. What does the name of the cat, Pluto, in the short story, "The Black Cat" imply?

2. "Who has not, a hundred times, found himself doing wrong, doing some evil thing for no other reason than because he knows he should not? Are not we humans at all times pushed, ever driven in some unknown way to break the law just because we understand it to be the law?"

   What does the author try to suggest the above passage?

   a. human's wickedness   b. human's righteousness
   c. human's goodness   d. human's helplessness

Exercise

* Choose the closest meaning to the underlined.

1. Our friendship lasted, in this manner, for several years.
   a. ended　b. continued　c. terminated　d. finished

2. Some students have great difficulty figuring out what to major in at college.
   a. estimating　b. understanding　c. choosing　d. approaching

3. Do you prefer coffee or tea?
   a. purchase　b. like　c. enjoy　d. arrange

4. Poe's appeal is not confined strictly to American readers.
   a. speech-applied　b. talent-limited
   c. fame-applied　d. attraction-limited

* Correct the underlined.

1. I alone fed the cat now.

2. We eat the food yesterday.

3. I hanged my clothes.

5-2.

Oedipus

King Laius of Thebes, was the third in descent from Cadmus. He married a distant cousin, Jocasta. With their reign[1] Apollo's oracle at Delphi began to play a leading part in the family's fortunes.

Apollo was the God of Truth. Whatever the priestess at Delphi said would happen infallibly came to pass. To attempt to act in such a way that the prophecy would be made void[2] was as futile as to set oneself against the decrees[3] of fate.[4] Nevertheless, when the oracle warned Laius that he would die at the hands of his son he determined that this should not be. When the child was born he bound its feet together and had it exposed on a lonely mountain where it must soon die. He felt no more fear; he was sure that on this point

---

1 reign 통치

2 the prophecy would be made void 예언이 무효가 되다

3 as futile as to set oneself against the decrees 스스로 천명(명령)에 대항하게 하는 것만큼 쓸모없는

4 According to Bulfinch, Laius "therefore committed the child to the care of a herdsman with orders to destroy him; but the herdsman, moved with pity, yet not daring entirely to disobey, tied up the child by the feet and left him hanging to the branch of a tree. In this condition the infant was found by a peasant, who carried him to his master and mistress, by whom he was adopted and called Oedipus, or Swollen-foot." (*Mythology: The Age of Fable*, p. 128)

he could foretell the future better than the god. His folly was not brought home to him. He was killed, indeed, but he thought the man who attacked him was a stranger. He never knew that in his death he had proved Apollo's truth.

When he died he was away from home and many years had passed since the baby had been left on the mountain. It was reported that a band of robbers had slain him together with his attendants, all except one, who brought the news home. The matter was not carefully investigated because Thebes was in sore straits[5] at the time. The country around was beset by a frightful monster, the Sphinx, a creature shaped like a winged lion, but with the breast and face of a woman. She lay in wait for the wayfarers along the roads to the city and whomever she seized she put a riddle to, telling him if he could answer it, she would let him go. No one could, and the horrible creature devoured man after man until the city was in a state of siege.[6] The seven great gates were the Thebans' pride remained closed, and famine drew near to the citizens.

So matters stood when there came into the stricken country a stranger, a man of great courage and great intelligence, whose name was Oedipus. He had left his home, Corinth, where he was held to be the son of the King, Polybus, and the reason for his self-exile was another Delphic oracle. Apollo had declared that he was fated to kill his father. He, too, like Laius, thought to make it impossible for the oracle to come true; he resolved never to see Polybus again. In his lonely wanderings he came into the country around Thebes and he heard what was happening there. He was a homeless, friendless man to whom life meant little and he determined to seek the Sphinx out and try to solve the riddle.

---

5 was in sore straits 극심한 곤란에 처해 있었다
6 in a state of siege 끈질기게 공격당하는 상태에

"What creature," the Sphinx asked him, "goes on four feet in the morning, on two at noonday, on three in the evening?"

"Man," answered Oedipus. "In childhood he creeps on hands and feet; in manhood he walks erect; in old age he helps himself with a staff." It was the right answer. The Sphinx, inexplicably, but most fortunately, killed herself; the Thebans were saved. Oedipus gained all and more than he had left. The grateful citizens made him their King and he married the dead King's wife, Jocasta. For many years they lived happily. It seemed that in this case Apollo's words had been proved to be false.

But when their two sons had grown to manhood Thebes was visited by a terrible plague. A blight[7] fell upon everything. Not only were men dying throughout the country, the flocks and herds and the fruits of the field were blasted[8] as well. Those who were spared death by disease faced death by famine. No one suffered more than Oedipus. He regarded himself as the father of the whole state; the people in it were his children; the misery of each one was his too. He dispatched Jocasta's brother Creon to Delphi to implore the god's help.

Creon returned with good news. Apollo had declared that the plague would be stayed upon one condition: whoever had murdered King Laius must be punished. Oedipus was enormously relieved. Surely the men or the man could be found even after all these years, and they would know well how to punish him. He proclaimed to the people gathered to hear the message Creon brought back.

Oedipus took the matter in hand with energy. He sent for Teiresias, the

7 blight 질병
8 were blasted 시들다, 해를 입다

old blind prophet, the most revered of Thebans. Had he any means of finding out, he asked him, who the guilty were? To his amazement and indignation the seer[9] at first refused to answer. "For the love of God," Oedipus implored him.

"If you have knowledge..." "Fools," Teiresias said. "Fools all of you. I will not answer."

But when Oedipus went so far as to accuse him of keeping silence because he had himself taken part in the murder, the prophet in his turn was angered and words he had meant never to speak fell heavily from his lips: "You are yourself the murderer you seek." To Oedipus the old man's mind was wandering; what he said was sheer madness. He ordered him out of his sight and never again to appear before him.

Jocasta too treated the assertion with scorn. "Neither prophets nor oracles have any sure knowledge," she said. She told her husband how the priestess at Delphi had prophesied that Laius should die at the hand of his son and how he and she together had seen to it that[10] this should not happen by having the child killed. "And Laius was murdered by robbers, where three roads meet on the way to Delphi," she concluded triumphantly. Oedipus gave her a strange look.

"When did this happen?" he asked slowly.

"Just before you came to Thebes," she said.

"How many were with him?" Oedipus asked.

"They were five in all," Jocasta spoke quickly, "all killed but one."

"I must see that man," he told her. "Send for him."

"I will," she said. "At once. But I have a right to know what is in your

9 seer 예언자
10 see to it that ~하도록 조처하다

mind."

"You shall know all that I know," he answered. "I went to Delphi just before I came here because a man had flung it in my face that I was not the son of Polybus. I went to ask the god. He did not answer me, but he told me horrible things—that I should kill my father, marry my mother, and have children men would shudder to look upon. I never went back to Corinth. On my way from Delphi, at a place where three roads met, I came upon a man with four attendants. He tried to force me from the path; he struck me with his stick. Angered I fell upon them and I killed them. Could it be the leader was Laius?" "The one man left alive brought back a tale of robbers," Jocasta said, "Laius was killed by robbers, not by his son—the poor innocent who died upon the mountain."

As they talked a further proof seemed given them that Apollo could speak falsely. A messenger came from Corinth to announce to Oedipus the death of Polybus. "O oracle of the god," Jocasta cried, "where are you now? The man died, but not by his son's hand." The messenger smiled wisely. "Did the fear of killing your father drive you from Corinth?" he asked.

"Ah, King, you were in error. You never had reason to fear—for you were not the son of Polybus. He brought you up as though you were his, but he took you from my hands."

"Where did you get me?" Oedipus asked. "Who were my father and mother?"

"I know nothing of them," the messenger said. "A wandering shepherd gave you to me, a servant of Laius."

Jocasta turned white; a look of horror was on her face.

"Why waste a thought upon what such a fellow says?" she cried. "Nothing he says can matter." She spoke hurriedly, yet fiercely.

Oedipus could not understand her. "My birth does not matter?" he asked.

"For God's sake, go no further," she said. "My misery is enough." She broke away and rushed into the palace.

At that moment an old man entered. He and the messenger eyed each other curiously. "The very man, O King," the messenger cried. "The shepherd who gave you to me."

"And you," Oedipus asked the other, "do you know him as he knows you?"

The old man did not answer, but the messenger insisted. "You must remember. You gave me once a little child you had found—and the King here is that child."

"Curse you," the other muttered. "Hold your tongue."

"What!" Oedipus said angrily. "You would conspire[11] with him to hide from me what I desire to know? There are ways, be sure, to make you speak."

The old man wailed, "Oh, do not hurt me. I did give him the child, but do not ask more, master, for the love of God."

"If I have to order you a second time to tell me where you got him, you are lost," Oedipus said.

"Ask your lady," the old man cried. "She can tell you best."

"She gave him to you?" asked Oedipus.

"Oh, yes, oh, yes," the other groaned. "I was to kill the child. There was a prophecy-"

"A prophecy!" Oedipus repeated. "That he should kill his father?"

"Yes," the old man whispered.

11 conspire 공모하다, 음모를 꾸미다

A cry of agony came from the King. At last he understood.

"All true! Now shall my light be changed to darkness. I am accursed."[12] He had murdered his father, he had married his father's wife, his own mother. There was no help for him, for her, for their children. All were accursed.

Within the palace Oedipus wildly sought for his wife that was his mother. He found her in her chamber. She was dead. When the truth broke upon her, she had killed herself. Standing beside her, he too turned his hand against himself, but not to end his life. He changed his light to darkness. He put out his eyes. The black world of blindness was a refuge; better to be there than to see with strange shamed eyes the old world that had been so bright.[13]

-Adapted from *Mythology* (pp. 256-61)

---

12 accursed[əkə:rsid] 저주받은

13 Thomas Bulfinch describes the end of the story as the following: "Jocasta put an end to her own life, and Oedipus, seized with madness, tore out his eyes and wandered away from Thebes, dreaded and abandoned by all except his daughters, who faithfully adhered to him, till after a tedious period of miserable wandering he found the termination of his wretched life." (129)

Exercise

* Choose the closest meaning of the underlined.

1. She <u>cast</u> herself down from the rock and perished.
   a. throw　　b. threw　　c. drown　　d. drowned

2. Not one had yet <u>succeed</u>ed in solving it.
   a. Will Charles succeed to the throne?
   b. If you want to succeed in your life, keep reading and learn!
   c. Four of his sons would eventually in turn succeed to his title.
   d. He succeeded to the throne on the death of his father.

3. My <u>misery</u> is enough.
   a. plague　　b. famine　　c. misfortune　　d. fortune

4. Jocasta <u>put an end to</u> her own life.
   a. stopped　　b. continued　　c. bore　　d. tortured

5. Apollo had <u>declared</u> that the plague would be stayed upon one condition.
   a. proclaimed　　b. relieved　　c. prophesied　　d. concluded

6. <u>Famine</u> drew near to the citizens.
   a. Female　　b. Starvation　　c. Fame　　d. Fear

7. Oedipus <u>resolved</u> never to see Polybus again.
   a. came　　b. determined　　c. proved　　d. grew

* Answer the questions.

1. Why did Oedipus put out his eyes?
   a. He didn't know what he is and what he has done.
   b. He made her wife kill herself.
   c. He wanted to be like the prophet, Teiresias.
   d. He wanted to be aided by his daughters.

2. What proverb could we recall, relating with the Oedipus story?
   a. All is well that ends well.
   b. Know your self.
   c. Forewarned is forearmed.
   d. Do not ask which is the right way to the blind.

3. Find the suitable proverb concerned with the theme of the above myth.
   a. Know yourself.
   b. Yesterday is the enemy of Today.
   c. Don't deceive yourself.
   d. Great boast, small roast.

Unit 6

6-1. *Arabian Nights*

6-2. *Snow White*

6-1.

Arabian Nights

The Sultan and Sheherezade

Sultan[1] Shahriar had a beautiful wife. She was his only wife, and he loved her more than anything in the world. Some people said that he loved her too much, and perhaps they were right, because she was not as good as she seemed. The sultan's love was not enough for her, and she turned to other men. One day he found her with a slave.

He cut off both their heads with his own sword.

From that day the sultan changed. Once he had loved one woman. Now he hated all women. "I can't be sure of any of them," he said to his vizir.[2] "From this time I shall marry a new wife every day, and at sunrise the next morning she must die. One day will not be long enough, even for a woman, to

1 Originally, it was an Arabic language abstract noun meaning "strength", "authority", "rulership" derived from the verbal noun sulṭah, meaning "authority" or "power." Later, it came to be used as the title of certain rulers who claimed almost full sovereignty in practical terms (i.e., the lack of dependence on any higher ruler), without claiming the overall caliphate, or to refer to a powerful governor of a province within the caliphate. The term is gradually being replaced by king.

2 vizier. (Ar.) (이슬람국, 특히 옛 터키 제국의) 고관, 장관

do wrong."

A time of great unhappiness then began for the sultan's people. Every family lived in fear. If the sultan asked a father for his daughter as a wife, how could the father say no? They began to hide their daughters, or send them into the country. It soon became difficult for the vizir to find new wives, and this made him afraid.

"What will the sultan do to me when I can't find any at all?" he thought.

Now, the vizir himself had two daughters. He was a good, loving father, and they did not like to see him look unhappy. One day, the elder, Sheherezade, said: "Father, I want you to do something for me. By doing this you will please the sultan, the people and me."

"In the name of God," said the vizir, "I would do anything to please so many people. Ask, and I will do it for you."

"Give me to the sultan as a wife."

The vizir's face turned white. "Give you up to be killed? Never! You don't know what you are saying."

"Father," said Sheherezade. "Are you a true servant of God, or do you use words without thinking? You can't say no. You said 'In the name of God,' so you must do this for me. I want to be the sultan's wife."

The vizir beat his head with his hands. He knew he had to do this thing. But why did she want to throw her life away?

Sheherezade went to her sister, Dunyazade, and told her what she had done. At first her sister wept, but Sheherezade kissed her and said: "Don't think I want to die. By this marriage I hope to save many girls' lives, and my own, too. But you must help me. I want you to sleep in the same room as the sultan and myself. Wake me up one hour before sunrise and ask me to tell you a story. That is only thing I ask."

The next day Sheherezade went with her father to see the sultan. The sultan was pleased and surprised. He never thought his vizir would give his own daughter as a wife. But there she was. Everything was made ready, and they were married.

That night, when it was time to go to bed, Sheherezade said: "My lord, my sister has always slept in the same room as me. May she stay with me tonight—my last night?"

"She can do as you wish," said the sultan. He was still pleased that the vizir had given him his own daughter.

Nobody slept that night. The sultan always slept badly. Sheherezade was excited. Dunyazade was afraid. She knew she had to stay awake to save her sister's life. One hour before sunrise she spoke: "Dear sister," she said, "if you are still awake, please tell me a story."

So Sheherezade began to tell stories such as "The man who never laughed again," "Ali Baba and the forty thieves," "Aladdin and the magic lamp," etc. The interesting story each night makes Sheherezade's life extend another day.

Exercise

* Circle the words in each of the following sentences that give clues to the meaning of the underlined vocabulary item. Then circle the letter of the word that gives the correct meaning of the item.

1. Television can increase our knowledge of the outside world; there are many high-quality programs that help us understand many fields of study: science, medicine, the arts, and so on.

   a. life b. understanding c. size

2. Children who view a lot of TV can often concentrate on a subject for only fifteen to twenty minutes; they can pay attention only for the amount of time between TV commercials!

   view: a. watch b. enjoy c. need

   concentrate: a. enjoy b. understand c. pay attention

3. To many people, television becomes more real than reality, and their own lives seem boring because they are not as exciting as the lives of actors on TV.

   reality: a. real life b. programs c. the present moment

   boring: a. exciting b. not interesting c. worried

4. A child begins to believe there is nothing strange about fights, killings, and other kinds of violence.

   a. mysteries that detectives can't solve

   b. actions that hurt people physically

   c. arguments between people

5. The most negative effect of television might be some people's strong addiction to it. They feel a strange and powerful need to watch it even when they don't enjoy it.
   a. enjoyment of   b. dislike of   c. need for

6. Addiction to TV is similar to drug or alcohol dependence: people almost never believe they are addicted. The "cure" is to throw away the TV—or to cut the cord with scissors.
   addicted: a. intelligent   b. dependent   c. dissatisfied
   cure: a. solution   b. disease   c. reality

7. Do you believe that your life will be more exciting and happier if you buy the products that you see on TV commercials?
   products: a. drugs or alcohol   b. things for sale   c. benefits
   commercials: a. exciting shows   b. violent movies   c. breaks in the programs

6-2.
Snow White

Once upon a time long ago a queen was sitting in her room. Outside the window it was snowing. She often looked outside at the snow. She was thinking about babies. She thought to herself: 'If only I could have a beautiful child, I want a child with skin as white as the snow. Hair as black as ebony.[1] And cheeks as red as apples!'

Soon after, the queen had a baby. The child had black hair, white skin and red cheeks. She was very pretty. She was named Snow White.

The queen died when the baby was born. The king was very sad, but he needed a new wife. He thought a baby should have a mother and a father.

One year later he married again. The new queen was very beautiful, but she was cold as ice. The queen was very proud of her beauty and wanted to be the most beautiful woman in the land. She did not like other beautiful women.

The queen had a special magic mirror. It could answer questions truthfully. The queen kept it on a wall, and she looked into it every day.

---

1 ebony 흑단(감나무과에 속한 상록 교목)

"Mirror, mirror, on the wall,

who's the fairest of them in the world?"

She always asked. Every time the mirror would say:

"You are the fairest of them all, my queen."

The queen was happy with its answer.

Snow White was a pretty, happy child. She was very sweet. She loved to laugh and play. The years passed, and Snow White was growing into a beautiful young woman. The queen was not happy. One day she stood in front of the mirror.

"Mirror, mirror, who's the fairest of them all?" she asked it.

"Queen, yesterday you were the most beautiful. Now, Snow White is the fairest," the mirror said. The queen was very angry and her face turned purple. She thought about the problem day and night. Her heart turned cold and hateful. She came to hate Snow White.

A few weeks later, the queen thought of a plan. She sent for a hunter. She told him to take Snow White deep into the woods and then kill her.

She asked him to bring back Snow White's heart. She wanted to make sure he followed her wishes. The hunter had to do what his queen asked. He agreed to her plan.

The next day, the hunter came to get Snow White. They went across the palace bridge and along the river to the woods. Snow White was a wise girl. She saw the hunter's big sword. She asked the hunter many questions, and she finally understood his plan.

"Please don't kill me! I will run away far into the woods and never return. I will forget I had a home here," she told him. Because she was so beautiful, his heart softened. He agreed to let her go. He thought wild animals would soon kill her, but he was glad he had not (to kill her).

After the girl ran away, the hunter saw a wild pig. He quickly killed it and took its heart.

Snow White ran through the woods. Suddenly she saw a small house in the middle of the woods. She was so tired and went closer to it. She knocked on the door but no one answered. Slowly she walked in.

There were seven small, low beds near the wall of the house. She wanted to sleep on the first bed, but it was too hard. She tried another one, but it was too soft.

The house was the home of seven small men, dwarves.

One day the queen went to her mirror on the wall.

"Mirror, mirror, who's the fairest of them all?"

"Snow White is still the most beautiful of all."

The queen was very angry. "Where is Snow White?"

"She stays with seven dwarves deep in the woods near seven mountains."

Soon she had an idea.

One afternoon, as Snow White was busy cleaning the floor, she heard a knock on the door. She looked out of the window and from behind a curtain she saw an ugly old woman holding a basket of goods.

"Hello! what are you selling?"

"I'm a poor old woman trying to make a bit of money. Today I'm selling pretty blue pieces of lace or nice orange belts, to tie up your skirts with. Blue would be very becoming on you."

The girl thought to herself, 'It is only a poor old woman. She will not hurt me.' And so she opened the door to let her in. The woman, who was really the queen, came in.

"Here, my dear, I'll help you tie it around your waist."

She tied it tighter and tighter until Snow White couldn't breathe. She dropped onto the floor. The queen thought she had killed her and she went away.

"Now I am again the most beautiful woman in the land!" she said to herself.

A week later Snow White was dreaming about a handsome man; wishing she could meet someone she could love.

One day he saw a young lady walking toward her, smiling. At first, Snow White was too afraid to speak to her, because of the dwarves' warning. But then Snow White thought to herself, 'This woman is young. She could not hurt me.' The woman stopped.

"Please, Miss, look at the beautiful brushes and combs I carry. They are cheap; only a dollar."

As soon as she paid, the woman said, "Now let me comb your hair for you." But the comb had poison on the end of it, and as soon as it touched Snow White's head she dropped to the ground. The young woman, of course, was the queen. She bent down beside Snow White and listened for her breath. She felt no air on her cheek. The queen was pleased that her plan had not failed and she went away.

Luckily, the dwarves came home soon after the queen left. The dwarves ran to her with heavy hearts when they saw Snow White lying on the ground. Then they saw the comb in her hair and they took it out. Soon she opened her eyes, but she was very weak.

Before long, the queen found out that Snow White still lived. 'Snow White is not dead yet, but this time I will not fail!'

This time she took an apple. One half of the apple was red, and the other was green. She put poison on the red half and kept the green part free of poison. She again dressed up like an old woman. She acted like she was blind. The queen visited the house in which Snow White lived.

"Please go away. I can't let anyone into the house."

"I won't come in. I'm selling these fine, sweet apples. Here, taste one first and then decide if you want to buy it. I will pass it to you through the window."

Snow White thought: 'I'm sorry. I promised my friends I must be very careful about buying things from strangers.'

But the queen was clever. "Look. I will take a bite from the apple. You will see that it can not harm you." She took a bite from the green side of the apple. Snow White felt sorry for the old blind woman, and the apple looked quite delicious to her. The queen passed the apple to Snow White through the window.

She bit into the red part and then fell to the floor. She lay there, not moving. The queen thought 'She will never move again. The dwarves cannot help her this time!' She quickly left.

When the dwarves arrived home, they found Snow White. "Oh, no! Snow White is surely dead this time!" They knew there was no hope when she would not wake up.

After a few days, they put her under a glass box. They did not want to cover her beautiful face. Snow White lay there over the two seasons of winter and spring.

One day in early summer a prince rode into the woods on a horse. He was very handsome and strong. The prince happened to see a glass box in the woods.

"How beautiful she is! How peaceful and gentle she looks!" The prince wanted to take her with him. The prince's men began to walk, and one of them tripped over a small tree. The box was shaken, and the piece of apple that was stuck in Snow White's throat came out.

Snow White began to breathe again. The prince and his men put box down with excitement and opened the glass. Snow White sat up and said, "Where am I? Who are you?" "I am a prince. I want you to be my wife. Will you come with me and marry me?"

Snow White could see that he had a gentle and kind heart. She fell in love with him.

Snow White and the prince planned a large, splendid wedding.

On the wedding day, the queen was getting ready. She wanted to wear something special, and so she put on beautiful purple clothes. She went and stood in front of the mirror and asked it, "Mirror, mirror, who's the fairest one of all?" The mirror said, "Queen, you were the fairest yesterday. But the prince's bride is now more beautiful than you."

The queen was very angry. She went to the wedding with her husband, the king. The queen wondered who's the prince's new bride was. When they entered the palace, they heard beautiful music. Hundreds of people were there. When the queen saw that it was Snow White, she was so shocked she could not move. She stands in the same place to this day.

Exercise

* Choose the closest meaning to the underlined.

1. You are the <u>fairest</u> of them all.
   a. ugliest b. prettiest c. righteous d. justness

2. The house was the home of seven <u>small men</u>.
   a. blinds b. dummies c. dwarves d. mummies

3. <u>Before long</u>, the queen found out that Snow White still lived.
   a. Then b. Therefore c. Furthermore d. Soon

* Correct the underlined.

1. She <u>bite</u> into the red part and then fell to the floor.

2. The prince's <u>bridegroom</u> is now more beautiful than you.

* Discuss the following.

1. Narcism

2. Jealousy

3. Aging is the enemy of beauty.

4. Feminism: Some people say this fairy tale shows a typical man-centered viewpoint.

Unit 7

7-1.

Art and Poverty

As a general rule, artists throughout the ages have been rather poverty-stricken.[1] Art and poverty seem to go hand in hand. Some of the best art has been produced in the midst of terrible want.[2] It is questionable whether poverty makes a man turn to art to forget his hunger or whether the man is poor because he is an artist. But in other case, the artist tries to overcome his poverty and devote himself to his art. Many artists do not become famous until after they are dead and buried. It is said that a prophet is never recognized in his own country.[3] A similar thing is true of the artist. Frequently his genius is recognized by strangers[4] before his own countrymen are aware of his extraordinary talent.

The present day[5] has seen the rise of a new type of art. This art has

---

1 poverty-stricken 몹시 가난한, 가난에 찌든

2 in the midst of terrible want 지독한 궁핍(결핍, 빈곤) 속에서

3 a prophet is never recognized in his own country는 "고향에서 환영받는 선지자 없다"(A prophet has no honor in his own country)라는 속담과 비슷한 표현으로 "선지자는 대개 자기 조국 밖에서 존경을 받는다"는 뜻이다(고창석, 『레토릭 영어명언』, 한국학술정보(2013), 17쪽 참조.

4 strangers: foreigners

5 The present day: Now

departed from the classical love of graphic and literal representation. Modern art is not so much[6] concerned with portraying an object exactly as it appears to the eye as with capturing its soul. In order to do this, the modern artist paints abstractions. He tries to express only the essentials of the object he is painting. Picasso is a good example of a modern artist. His conception of things took the form of geometrical shapes.[7] Consequently, Picasso's art is called "cubism."[8]

The artistic trends of any given time are usually well reflected in the architecture of the period. The God-centered world of the Middle Ages found expression in massive cathedrals. The building of a cathedral was a labor of love in which most of the townspeople participated. Everyone contributed his skill to the building in order to express his religious belief and to pay homage to[9] God. The spirit of the modern business world is similarly reflected in the skyscraper.[10] The skyscraper, however, is not designed merely for utility. It combines practicality with grace and beauty. Modern man, in all his scientific advancement, has not lost his eye for beauty.

Expert : How do you like to go to the art museum this afternoon?

Layman: I'm afraid art is beyond me. When I look at a painting or a statue, I have a hard time[11] appreciating its beauty.

Expert : Have you ever really tried to understand art? It's not so difficult as it seems.

---

6 not so much A as B: A보다 차라리 B다. I'm not so much concerned with what you say as with how you act.

7 geometrical shapes 기하학적인 모습들

8 cubism 입체파

9 pay homage to ~에 경의를 나타내다

10 skyscraper 고층건물

11 have a hard time (in) doing something: have difficulty (in) doing ~하는데 애먹다. Most of Korean students have a hard time pronouncing some English sounds, [ð], [θ] in father, think.

Layman: That's a matter of opinion. I'm just not a born artist. Art leaves me cold.

Expert : Perhaps the current exhibition at the art museum would be just the thing[12] to kindle the spark of interest in you. Why not give it a try?

Layman: Is it a exhibition of the great masters?

Expert : On the contrary. It's an exhibition of modern art. The emphasis is on modern oil paintings.

Layman: You mean those things full of squares, cubes, and things?

Expert : Well yes, if you want to put it that way.

Layman: In that case, I'm sure I don't want to go. I can't make head or tail out of[13] modern art. It's too difficult to understand.

Expert : I used to think so too until I heard the story about "Palette" O'Toole.

Layman: Palette O'Toole? Never heard of him.

Expert : He used to be head of the Modern Art Society, but one of his paintings caused a scandal and he had to resign.

Layman: How come?[14]

Expert : He entered[15] an abstract painting in an exhibition of the Modern Art Society and won first prize.

Layman: I don't see anything scandalous about that.

Expert : But it was. You see, his painting wasn't really a painting. It was merely his paint-smeared[16] palette. O'Toole had entered it as a joke.

---

12 just the thing: suitable; exactly right. Since my uncle is sick, I think we ought to pay him a vist. It would be just the thing to cheer him up.

13 be unable to make head or tail out of: be unable to understand. This report is written so badly that I can't make head or tail out of it.

14 How come?: Why?

15 enter 출품하다

16 paint-smeared 물감으로 얼룩진

Layman: And the judges gave first prize to a palette? That must have caused them a lot of embarrassment.

Expert : It certainly did. The judges said that O'Toole had deliberately entered his palette in the exhibition just to make fools of them.

Layman: It looks as if he succeeded. Is that why he had to resign?

Expert : Yes. But the point I'm trying to make is that you needn't understand modern art to appreciate it.

Layman: But if you can't understand modern art, what's the use of[17] looking at it?

Expert : It's hard to explain. There are some paintings that you like instinctively. I enjoy them just for their colors and design.

Layman: Maybe I should go along with you this afternoon.

Expert : Yes. It'll be a good experience for you. Who knows, you may find yourself becoming fond of modern art.

Layman: I doubt it. But I'm willing to give it a try.

Expert : That's the spirit.[18] You may find there's more to modern art than meets the eye.

Layman: Perhaps I should buy a palette and enter it in the next exhibition. A few dabs[19] of paint here and there might bring me a blue ribbon.[20]

Expert : In your case, I think you'd be more likely[21] to get a black eye.[22]

---

17 what's the use of 무슨 소용이야. what profit is there. What's the use of taking lessons if you don't study?

18 That's the spirit. 그래야지(그런 정신이어야지).

19 dabs 가볍게 두드리듯이 채색하는 것

20 blue ribbon: first prize

21 more likely to ~할 것 같다. You're more likely to become good at English if you try to speak it every day.

22 get a black eye 눈언저리를 얻어맞아 퍼렇게 멍들다. 일종의 pun(동음이의의 익살)으로 blue에 대한 black을 사용하여 색깔에 관계시켜 표현했다.

Exercise

A. In each column, which word does not belong? Cross it out.

1. kitchen	screen	porch	living room
2. coffee	lemonade	iced tea	strawberries
3. breeze	hot	cool	warm
4. housework	child care	gardening	social

B. Match each word on the left with its meaning on the right. Write the correct letter on the line.

1. ___ quiet	a. to come back
2. ___ boob tube	b. conversation about unimportant things
3. ___ stare	c. not talking; with no sound
4. ___ rock	d. television
5. ___ breeze	e. something to make a breeze
6. ___ fan	f. to wait or stop
7. ___ reappear	g. to move back and forth
8. ___ pause	h. to look at
9. ___ argue	i. a small wind
10. ___ small talk	j. to fight; not to agree

C. Translate the following into Korean.

1. The artistic trends of any given time are usually well reflected in the architecture of the period.

2. I'm not an expert about painting, just a layman.

3. Perhaps the current exhibition at the art museum would be just the thing to kindle the spark of interest in you.

4. He used to be head of the Modern Art Society, but one of his paintings caused a scandal and he had to resign.

7-2.

A Definition of Art

—Herbert Read[1]

The simple word "art" is most usually associated with those arts which we distinguish as "plastic"[2] or "visual," but properly speaking it should include the arts of literature and music. There are certain characteristics common to all the arts, and though in these notes we are concerned only with the plastic arts, a definition of what is common to all the arts is the best starting-point of our enquiry.

It was Schopenhauer[3] who first said that all arts aspire to the condition of

1 Lee A. Jacobus, ed. *Aesthetics and the Arts* (New York: McGraw-Hill, 1968)에서 전재. Sir Herbert Edward Read (1893-1968)는 영국의 시인이자 비평가

2 plastic 조형적인

3 Arthur Schopenhauer (1788-1860) was a German philosopher best known for his book, *The World as Will and Representation*, in which he claimed that our world is driven by a continually dissatisfied will, continually seeking satisfaction. Influenced by Eastern philosophy, he maintained that the "truth was recognized by the sages of India"; consequently, his solutions to suffering were similar to those of Vedantic and Buddhist thinkers (e.g., asceticism). The influence of "transcendental ideality" led him to choose atheism. At age 25, he published his doctoral dissertation, *On the Fourfold Root of the Principle of Sufficient Reason*, which examined the four distinct aspects of experience in the phenomenal world; consequently, he has been influential in the history of phenomenology. He has influenced many thinkers, including Friedrich Nietzsche, Richard Wagner, Adolf Hitler, Ludwig Wittgenstein, Erwin Schrödinger, Albert Einstein, Sigmund Freud, Otto Rank, Carl Jung, Joseph Campbell, Leo Tolstoy, Thomas Mann,

music; that remark has often been repeated, and has been the cause of a good deal of misunderstanding, but it does express an important truth. Schopenhauer was thinking of the abstract qualities of music; in music, and almost in music alone, it is possible for the artist to appeal to his audience directly, without the intervention of a medium of communication in common use for other purposes. The architect must express himself in buildings which have some utilitarian[4] purpose. The poet must use words which are bandied[5] about in the daily give-and-take of conversation. The painter must express himself by the representation of the visible world. Only the composer of music is perfectly free to create a work of art out of his own consciousness, and with no other aim than to please. But all artists have this same intention, the desire to please; and art is most simply and most usually defined as an attempt to create pleasing forms. Such forms satisfy our sense of beauty and the sense of beauty is satisfied when we are able to appreciate a unity of harmony of formal relations among our sense-perceptions.

Any general theory of art must *begin* with this supposition: that man responds to the shape and surface and mass of things present to his sense, and that certain arrangements in the proportion of the shape and surface and mass of things result in a pleasurable sensation, whilst the lack of such arrangement leads to indifference or even to positive discomfort and revulsion.[6] The sense of pleasurable relations is the sense of beauty; the opposite sense is the sense of ugliness. It is possible, of course, that some people are quite unaware of proportions in the physical aspect of things. Just as some people are

---

and Jorge Luis Borges, among others.

4 utilitarian 공리적인, 실용적인

5 bandy 서로 주고받다

6 revulsion (감정의) 격변, 급변

color-blind, so others may be blind to shape and surface and mass. But just as people who are color-blind are comparatively rare, so there is every reason to believe that people wholly unaware of the other visible properties of objects are equally rare. They are more likely to be undeveloped.

There are at least a dozen current definitions of beauty, but the merely physical one I have already given (beauty is a unity of formal relations among our sense-perceptions) is the only essential one, and from this basis we can build up a theory of art which is as inclusive as any theory of art need be. But it is perhaps important to emphasize at the outset[7] the extreme relativity of this term beauty. The only alternative is to say that art has no necessary connection with beauty—a perfectly logical position to hold if we confine the term to that concept of beauty established by the Greeks and continued by the classical tradition in Europe. My own preference is to regard the sense of beauty as a very fluctuating[8] phenomenon, with manifestations in the course of history that are very uncertain and often very baffling.[9] Art should include all such manifestations, and the test of a serious student of art is that, whatever his own sense of beauty, he is willing to admit into the realm of art the genuine manifestations[10] of that sense in other people at other periods. For him, Primitive, Classical and Gothic are of equal interest, and he is not so much concerned to assess[11] the relative merits of such periodical manifestations of the sense of beauty as to distinguish between the genuine and false of all periods.

Most of our misconceptions of art arise from a lack of consistency in the

---

7 at the outset 처음부터, 시작부터

8 fluctuating 변동하는, 오르내리는

9 baffling[bǽfəliŋ] 당황케 하는; 이해할 수 없는(inscrutable)

10 genuine manifestations 진실한 선언들

11 assess 평가하다

use of the words art and beauty. It might be said that we are only consistent in our misuse of them. We always assume that all that is beautiful is art, or that all art is beautiful, that what is not beautiful is not art, and that ugliness is the negation of art. This identification of art and beauty is at the bottom of all our difficulties in the appreciation of art, and even in people who are acutely sensitive to aesthetic impressions in general, this assumption acts like an unconscious censor[12] in particular cases when art is not beauty. For art is not necessarily beauty: that cannot be said too often or too blatantly.[13] Whether we look at the problem historically or sociologically we find that art often has been or often is a thing of no beauty.

Beauty is sometimes defined simply as that which gives pleasure; and thus people are driven into admitting that eating and smelling and other physical sensation can be regarded as arts. Though this theory can quickly be reduced to absurdity, a whole school of aesthetics is founded on it, and until lately this school was even the predominant one. It has now been superseded[14] in the main[15] by a theory of aesthetics derived from Benedetto Croce,[16] and though Croce's theory has met with a flood of criticism, its general tenet,[17] that art is perfectly defined when simply defined as *intuition*, has proved to be much more illuminating than any previous theory. The difficulty has been to apply a theory depending on such vague terms as "intuition" and "lyricism." But the point to note immediately is, that this elaborate and inclusive theory of the arts gets on very well[18] without the word "beauty."

---

12 like an unconscious censor 무의식적인 비평가(검열자)처럼

13 blatantly 소란스럽게, 노골적으로

14 superseded 대신해왔다

15 in the main 주로, 대개

16 Benedetto Croce (1866-1952) 이탈리아의 이상주의 철학가

17 tenet 주의(主義), 교의(教義)(doctrine)

The concept of beauty is, indeed, of limited historical significance. It arose in ancient Greece and was the offspring of a particular philosophy of life. That philosophy was anthropomorphic[19] in kind; it exalted all human values and saw in the gods nothing but man writ large.[20] Art, as well as religion, was an idealization of nature, and especially of man as the culminating point[21] of the process of nature. The type of classical art is the Apollo Belvedere[22] or the Aphrodite of Melos[23]—perfect or ideal types of humanity, perfectly formed, perfectly proportioned, noble and serene;[24] in one word, beautiful. This type of beauty was inherited by Rome, and revived at the Renaissance.[25] We still live in

---

18 this elaborate and inclusive theory of the arts gets on very well 이 정교하고 포괄적인 예술이론은 매우 잘 진행되고 있다.

19 anthropomorphic 의인화(인격화)된. cf. anthropo- '사람, 인류(학)'의 뜻의 결합사이고 morph는 형태란 뜻이다.

20 nothing but man writ large 단지 인간을 크게 서술한

21 culminating point 정점, 최고점

22 Apollo Belvedere: Vatican에 있는 조형미의 전형으로 여겨지는 고대 조각품

23 Aphrodite of Melos: Venus of Milo. 아프로디테는 그리스 신화의 미의 여신으로 로마신화의 Venus와 같다.

24 serene 평온한

25 The birth of an incredible period of history we call the Renaissance. In fact, everywhere you look in Italy, you can find reminders of the Renaissance and its impact on the modern world.

By the late 1300s, Italy was enjoying a time of health and wealth. Nobody really worried about war and survival. They began to be interested in the future and paid more attention to the arts. By 1434, powerful families, like the Medici family, ruled Italian cities.

Italy grew in wealth and fame, and soon became the center of art, literature, and culture in Europe.

In the past, the work of great scholars and artists mainly dealt with ideas about God. But during the Renaissance, many people became interested in the art of the ancient Greeks and Romans. A new, original, way of thinking was born, focused on humans themselves.

In this time, Italian artists created extraordinary art that showed the beauty of man and nature, and the challenges of the human experience. One of these artists, Michelangelo, completed the lovely statue of David, and covered the Vatican's Sistine chapel with amazing stories and designs.

Then there was Leonardo da Vinci—artist, scientist, and inventor. To make his art feel more real, Leonardo studied the human body carefully. The facts he drew were both life-like and mysterious.

By the 1500s, Italy had become a model for the rest of Europe and other countries became

the tradition of the Renaissance, and for us beauty is inevitably associated with the idealization of a type of humanity evolved by an ancient people in a far land, remote from the actual conditions of our daily life. Perhaps as an ideal it is as good as any other; but we ought to realize that it is only one of several possible ideals. It differs from the Byzantine[26] ideal, which was divine rather than human, intellectual and anti-vital,[27] abstract. It differs from the Primitive ideal, which was perhaps no ideal at all, but rather a propitiation,[28] an expression of fear in the face of a mysterious and implacable[29] world. It differs also from the Oriental ideal, which is abstract too, nonhuman, metaphysical, yet instinctive rather than intellectual. But our habits of thought are so dependent on our outfit[30] of words, that we try, often enough in vain, to force this one word "beauty" into the service of all these ideals as expressed in art. If we are honest with ourselves, we are bound to feel guilty sooner or later of verbal

---

interested in building knowledge as well. For example, all over Europe, people wanted to know more about the world. So, they looked at science and reason for answers.

For example, the Polish astronomer Nicolaus Copernicus was the first to say that the Earth goes around the sun. Galileo Galilei, who invented the thermometer, was the first to use a telescope to look up at the skies, and saw that Copernicus's ideas were right.

It is great minds like Copernicus and Galileo that began the scientific revolution and a thirst for knowledge that has continued until our modern times. (*Reading Adventures 2*, Boston, MA: National Geographic Learning, 2013. p. 122.)

26 The Byzantine Empire, sometimes known as the Eastern Roman Empire, was the predominantly Greek-speaking continuation of the eastern half of the Roman Empire during Late Antiquity and the Middle Ages. Its capital city was Constantinople(modern-day Istanbul), originally founded as Byzantium. It survived the 5th century fragmentation and fall of the Western Roman Empire and continued to exist for an additional thousand years until it fell to the Ottoman Turks in 1453. During most of its existence, the empire was the most powerful economic, cultural, and military force in Europe. Both "Byzantine Empire" and "Eastern Roman Empire" are historiographical terms created after the end of the realm; its citizens continued to refer to their empire as the *Roman Empire* or Romania, and to themselves as "Romans."

27 anti-vital 반 활력적인

28 propitiation[prəpiʃieiʃən] 달램, 속죄

29 implacable 달래기 어려운; 용서 없는, 무자비한(relentless)

30 outfit 소양, 능력

distortion.[31] A Greek Aphrodite, a Byzantine Madonna[32] and a savage idol from New Guinea[33] or the Ivory Coast[34] cannot one and all[35] belong to this classical concept of beauty. The latter[36] at least, if words are to have any precise meaning, we must confess to be unbeautiful or ugly. And yet, whether beautiful or ugly, all these objects may be legitimately described as works of art.

Art, we must admit, is not the expression in plastic form of any one particular ideal. It is the expression of any ideal which the artist can realize in plastic form. And though I think that every work of art has some principle of form or coherent structure, I would not stress this element in any obvious sense, because the more one studies the structure of works of art which live in virtue of[37] their direct and instinctive appeal, the more difficult it becomes to reduce them to simple and explicable formulae.[38] That "there is no excellent beauty that hath[39] not some strangeness in the proportion" was evident even to a Renaissance moralist.

However we define the sense of beauty, we must immediately qualify it as theoretical; the abstract sense of beauty is merely the elementary basis of the artistic activity. The exponents[40] of this activity are living men and their activity

---

31 verbal distortion 언어적 왜곡(곡해, 견강부회(牽强附會))

32 Madonna (from Italian ma donna, meaning "my lady") most commonly refers to:
- Madonna, an appellation of Mary (mother of Jesus), a religious figure in Christianity and Islam
- Madonna (art), pictorial or sculptured representations of Mary, Mother of Jesus

33 New Guinea (Indonesian: Papua) is a large Island in the southwest Pacific Ocean. It is the world's second-largest island, after Greenland, covering a land area of 786,000 ㎢.

34 Ivory Coast or Côte d'Ivoire[ˌkʊt di'vwɑr], officially the Republic of Côte d'Ivoire, is a country in West Africa.

35 one and all 모조리

36 The latter(후자)는 confess의 목적어

37 in[by] virtue of ~의 힘으로, ~의 덕택으로

38 explicable formulae[fɔːrmjəliː] (*pl.* ~s, -lae) 설명(납득)할 수 있는 방식

39 hath: has의 옛날 표현

40 exponents[ikspounənt] 설명자, 해설자

is subject to all the cross-currents[41] of life. There are three stages: first, the mere perception of material qualities—colors, sounds, gestures, and many more complex and undefined physical reactions; second, the arrangement of such perceptions into pleasing shapes and patterns. The aesthetic sense may be said to end with these two processes, but there may be a third stage which comes when such an arrangement of perceptions is made to correspond with a previously existing or feeling is given *expression*. In this sense it is true to say that art is expression—nothing more and nothing less. But it is always necessary to remember that expression in this sense is a final process depending on the preceding processes of sensuous prcception and formal (pleasurable) arrangement. Expression can, of course, be completely devoid of formal arrangement, but then its very incoherence forbids us to call it art.

Aesthetics, or the science of perception, is only concerned with the first two processes; art may involve beyond these values of an emotional kind. It may be said that nearly all the confusion in the discussion of art arises from the failure to keep this distinction clear; ideas that concern only the history of art are introduced into discussions of the concept of beauty; the purpose of art, which is the communication of feeling, is inextricably confused with the quality of beauty,[42] which is the feeling communicated by particular forms.

The permanent element in mankind which corresponds to the element of form in art is man's aesthetic sensibility. It is the sensibility that is static. What is variable is the understanding which man builds up from the abstraction of his sensible impressions, his intellectual life, and to this we owe the variable element in art—that is to say, expression. I am not sure that "expression" is good word

41 is subject to all the cross-currents 반주류적 경향(상반되는 경향)에 지배받는다.

42 inextricably confused with the quality of beauty 해결할 수 없을 만큼 미의 특질이 혼란스러워진다.

to use in contrast to "form." Expression is used to denote natural emotional reactions, but the very discipline or restraint by which the artist achieves form is itself a mode of expression. Form, though it can be analyzed into intellectual terms like measure, balance, rhythm and harmony, is really intuitive in origin; it is not in the actual practice of artists in intellectual product. It is rather emotion directed and defined, and when we describe art as "the will to form" we are not imagining an exclusively intellectual activity, but rather an exclusively instinctive one. For this reason I do not think we can say that Primitive art is a lower form of beauty than Greek art, because although it may represent a lower kind of civilization, it may express an equal or even a finer instinct for form. The art of a period is a standard only so long as we learn to distinguish between the elements of form, which are universal, and the elements of expression, which are temporal. Still less can we say that in *form* Giotto[43] is inferior to Michelangelo.[44] He may be less complicated, but form is not valued for its degree of complexity. Frankly, I do not know how we are to judge form except by the same instinct that creates it.

43 Giotto di Bondone (1266–1337), known as Giotto, was an Italian painter and architect from Florence in the late Middle Ages. He is generally considered the first in a line of great artists who contributed to the Italian Renaissance.

44 Michelangelo di Lodovico Buonarroti Simoni (1475–1564), commonly known as Michelangelo (Italian pronunciation: [mikeˈlandʒelo]), was an Italian sculptor, painter, architect, poet, and engineer of the High Renaissance who exerted an unparalleled influence on the development of Western art. Despite making few forays beyond the arts, his versatility in the disciplines he took up was of such a high order that he is often considered a contender for the title of the archetypal Renaissance man, along with his fellow Italian Leonardo da Vinci.

Exercise

* Make each sentence using the following idiom or word(s).

1. devote oneself to art

2. portray: *The Portrait of Artist as a Young Man* by James Joyce, an Ireland novelist

3. Everyone contributed his skill to the building in order to express his religious belief and to pay homage to God.

4. exhibit

5. emphasize on

* Translate the underlined into Korean and explain them.

1. The <u>sense</u> of pleasurable relations is the sense of beauty; the opposite sense is the sense of ugliness.

2. Eating and smelling and other physical <u>sensation</u> can be regarded as arts.

3. In this <u>sense</u> it is true to say that art is expression—nothing more and nothing less.

4. Expression in this sense is a final process depending on the preceding processes of <u>sensuous</u> preception and formal (pleasurable) arrangement.

5. The permanent element in mankind which corresponds to the element of form in art is man's aesthetic sensibility.

6. Man builds up from the abstraction of his sensible impressions.

7. People are acutely sensitive to aesthetic impressions in general.

*** Translate the underlined into Korean.**

1. Though this theory can quickly be reduced to absurdity, a whole school of aesthetics is founded on it, and until lately this school was even the predominant one.

2. Art should include all such manifestations.

*** Fill in the blanks with appropriate word(s).**

1. Aesthetics is the science of ________.
   a. perception b. reality c. analysis d. communication

2. ________ is sometimes defined simply as that which gives pleasure.
   a. Misunderstanding b. Beauty c. Representation d. Supposition

Unit 8

8-1. *Music*

8-2. *East and West*

8-3. *As Rich as Croesus*

8-1.

Music

The homes of the world are made brighter by the music of thousands of radios and compact disc players. Even the silence of the forest is broken by the singing of birds. A man's love of music does not depend on education or social position. A peasant can be as deeply moved by a great symphony as a king. Music is the universal language.

In addition to giving enjoyment to thousands of individuals, music plays an important role in society. The armies of the world march to music. Formal occasions—graduations, openings of conventions, and the like—are dignified by the playing of music. Every country has its national anthem which stirs feelings of patriotism in the hearts of its listeners. Cities and towns have their colorful folk songs and ballads[1] which preserve the history and folklore[2] of the region. On occasions of great emotion, such as weddings and funerals, people find a natural outlet[3] for their feelings in songs of joy or sorrow.

1 ballads 민요
2 folklore 민담
3 find an outlet 출구를 찾다

Just as music is a universal language, so it is a mirror of the times. The God-centered thought of the Middle Ages found expression in hymns and chants of worship,[4] while the dignity and grace of the eighteenth century are reflected in stately minuets.[5] The new thought and romanticism of the nineteenth century were well portrayed by great masters such as Beethoven and Brahms. In a similar way, the modern age finds expression in the rhythms of jazz and swing. Even the music of the so-called modern "classical" composers is characterized by strange rhythms and discords.[6] A hundred years from now, people will listen to our music and get a taste of the restlessness and vigor of the present age.

A few years ago, most intellectuals scorned popular music. They thought it had little or no value. But today, people are becoming increasingly aware that jazz, swing, and the other forms of twentieth century music are a valid and worthwhile trend in music. Today, many colleges and universities hold classes in the history of jazz as part of American culture. But there are still some people who refuse to admit the value of jazz. Every family has a maiden aunt who looks down her nose at[7] the younger generation's interest in "that barbaric racket."[8] But she will listen with pleasure to some of the classical "racket" of men like Wagner.

---

4 hymn and chant of worship 성가

5 stately minuets 장엄한 미뉴에트

6 discords 부조화음

7 look down one's nose at: scorn, contempt. Don't look down your nose at me just because I don't have as much money as you.

8 barbaric racket 떠들썩한 것

8-2.

East and West

—Pearl S. Buck[1]

It has long been a fashion to say that the East is "spiritual" and the West is "material." But like many things that are carelessly said, it is not true. The East is neither more nor less spiritual than the West, and, the West is neither more nor less materialistic than the East. This may be said of all men alike: they prefer to have food rather than to starve, to have shelter than to be homeless, to be healthy rather than diseased, to live long rather than short lives, to be happy rather than sorrowful.

Then where did this myth about the spiritual East and the material West come from? It has its roots in a sort of truth, and this truth can be simply

1 Pearl Sydenstricker Buck (1892–1973), also known by her Chinese name Sai Zhenzhu (Chinese: 賽珍珠), was an American writer and novelist. As the daughter of missionaries, Buck spent most of her life before 1934 in China. Her novel *The Good Earth* was the best-selling fiction book in the U.S. in 1931 and 1932 and won the Pulitzer Prize in 1932. In 1938, she was awarded the Nobel Prize in Literature "for her rich and truly epic descriptions of peasant life in China and for her biographical masterpieces."

After her return to the United States in 1935, she continued her prolific writing career, and became a prominent advocate of the rights of women and minority groups, and wrote widely on Asian cultures, becoming particularly well known for her efforts on behalf of Asian and mixed race adoption.

stated: people in the East like to enjoy life. They will not work so hard that they have no time for simple pleasure in living, in eating, in sleeping, in playing with their children, and in talking with their wives and families. They will not take on[2] two jobs if they can pay their bills with one, for two jobs consume their time and distract their minds. They do not want to think constantly about work. But they are not in the least[3] lazy. They put an enormous amount of energy into their skills and pastimes. But to work merely to earn more money than they need is, to them, not sensible. They are ambitious but not, most of all, for money. All that they want cannot be bought with money. Peace cannot be bought with money and fun cannot be bought with money, nor laughter, nor time to smoke and drink tea, nor time to make flower gardens and write poetry or to walk on the hills carrying a bird cage.

To have more cars, more houses, better houses, finer furniture, more expensive clothes than one's neighbor has—these are desirable in the West, and money is needed to meet the desires. But the average man of the East knows that he cannot ride in more than one car at a time, nor live in more than one house at a time, nor sleep in more than one bed at a time. And he does not want other people to envy his well dressed wife and daughters, nor does he want to envy theirs. So why does he need so much money?

It is not that one man is more spiritual than the other, or more material. It is obvious that the values in the East and in the West are different. The man in the East wants more out of life itself than the man in the West does. If anything[4] the East is more materialistic than the West. The East, being so old,

---

2 take on: undertake, engage in

3 not in the least: not at all, never

4 If anything: rather(오히려), 어느 편인가 하면

knows how short life is. Man's years pass so soon. Therefore, enjoyment of life cannot be put off, for in old age the senses are dulled, and man can enjoy but a little. To waste one's youth, therefore, in making money would, to the man of the East, seem the merest folly.

People in the crowded countries of the East have lived so closely together that they know the happiness of all depends upon the happiness of the individual. Individuals can only be happy when they are allowed personal freedom inside the close human unit of family and community. Therefore, each individual must be dealt with by others as an individual. Grandfather has grandfather's needs. He is old and talkative, and somebody must listen to his talk and answer him and make him feel welcome and respected. And little grandson is not grown enough. So, he does not know how to behave yet, and so too much must not be expected of him. He must be taught, without frustrating him too much, that he must consider the needs of others, not only his own.

All this is done, not from a religious motive, but from plain common sense. Everybody is happier if all are happy, and the aim of life is to be as happy as one can be. The emphasis on human happiness is, I believe, the greatest gift which the East has for the West.

We of the West need to have happiness restored to us, not through a new religion, but through a simple return to those things which make people really happy. The East is right about it—what makes a human being happy is to feel himself wanted and understood and appreciated. The fabulous courtesy of the East is not a ritual, but simply oil to grease the machinery of human relationships.

And the people of the East need from us the physical aids which will make them still more happy—science to heal diseased bodies, to ease crushing toil,[5] and to provide more food.

There is nothing incomprehensible in the East or in the West. We are like men digging a tunnel through a mountain. We have begun at opposite ends, but the goal is the same—human happiness. We ought to meet somewhere one of these days and find that each faces the other's light.

—Adapted

5 crushing toil 엄청난 고생

Exercise

* Choose the opposite meaning(s) to the underlined.

1. Two jobs consume their time and distract their minds.
   a. pay–attract b. use–concentrate c. save–attract d. collect–concentrate

2. People put an enormous amount of energy into their skills and pastimes.
   a. huge–jobs b. little–amusements c. big–hobbies d. little–jobs

* Choose the closest meaning to the underlined.

1. Enjoyment of life cannot be put off.
   a. cancelled b. postponed c. limited d. bought

2. Each individual must be dealt with by others as an individual.
   a. exchanged b. traded c. treated d. respected

8-3.

As Rich as Croesus

This story comes from the Greek historian Herodotus. Croesus[1] (560–546 B.C.), king of Lydia in Asia Minor, was a ruler of proverbial[2] wealth. How Cyrus spared his life is a legendary example of mercy becoming the crown of justice. The story also offers important lessons about money and power's real bearing on happiness.

Some thousands of years ago there lived in Asia a king whose name was Croesus. The country over which he ruled was not very large, but its people were prosperous and famed for their wealth. Croesus himself was said to be the richest man in the world, and so well known is his name that, to this day, it is not uncommon to say of a very wealthy person that he is "as rich as Croesus."

King Croesus had everything that could make him happy—lands and houses and slaves, fine clothing to wear, and beautiful things to look at. He could not think of anything that he needed to make him more comfortable or

1 Croesus[kriːsəs] 크리서스(기원전 6세기의 Lydia 최후의 왕; 큰 부자로 유명); 큰 부자, (as) rich as ~ 굉장한 부호로

2 proverbial 소문난, 이름난

contented. "I am the happiest man in the world," he said.

It happened one summer that a great man from across the sea was traveling in Asia. The name of this man was Solon, and he was the lawmaker of Athens in Greece. He was noted for his wisdom and, centuries after his death, the highest praise that could be given to a learned man was to say, "He is as wise as Solon."

Solon had heard of Croesus, and so one day he visited him in his beautiful palace. Croesus was now happier and prouder than ever before, for the wisest man in the world was his guest. He led Solon through his palace and showed him the grand rooms, the fine carpets, the soft couches, the rich furniture, the pictures, the books. Then he invited him out to see his gardens and his orchards and his stables, and he showed him thousands of rare and beautiful things that he had collected from all parts of the world.

In the evening as the wisest of men and the richest of men were dining together, the king said to his guest, "Tell me now, O Solon, who do you think is the happiest of all men?" He expected that Solon would say, "Croesus."

The wise man was silent for a minute, and then he said, "I have in mind a poor man who once lived in Athens and whose name was Tellus. He, I doubt not, was the happiest of all men."

This was not the answer that Croesus wanted, but he hid his disappointment and asked, "Why do you think so?"

"Because," answered his guest, "Tellus was an honest man who labored hard for many years to bring up his children and to give them a good education. And when they were grown and able to do for themselves, he joined the Athenian army and gave his life bravely in the defense of his country. Can you think of anyone who is more deserving of happiness?"

"Perhaps not," answered Croesus, half choking with disappointment. "But who do you think ranks next to Tellus in happiness?" He was quite sure now that Solon would say, "Croesus."

"I have in mind," said Solon, "two young men whom I knew in Greece. Their father died when they were mere children, and they were very poor. But they worked manfully to keep the house together and to support their mother, who was in feeble health. Year after year they toiled, nor thought of anything but their mother's comfort. When at length she died, they gave all their love to Athens, their native city, and nobly served her as long as they lived."

Then Croesus was angry. "Why is it," he asked, "that you make me of no account and think that my wealth and power are nothing? Why is it that you place these poor working people above the richest king in the world?"

"O king," said Solon, "no man can say whether you are happy or not until you die. For no man knows what misfortunes may overtake you, or what misery may be yours in place of all this splendor."

Many years after this there arose in Asia a powerful king whose name was Cyrus. At the head of a great army he marched from one country to another, overthrowing many a kingdom and attaching it to his great empire of Babylon. King Croesus with all his wealth was not able to stand against this mighty warrior. He resisted as long as he could. Then his city was taken, his beautiful palace was burned, his orchards and gardens were destroyed, his treasures were carried away, and he himself was made prisoner.

"The stubbornness of this man Croesus," said King Cyrus, "has caused us much trouble and the loss of many good soldiers. Take him and make an example of him for other petty kings who may dare to stand in our way."

Thereupon[3] the soldiers seized Croesus and dragged him to the marketplace, handling him pretty roughly all the time. Then they built up a great pile of dry sticks and timber taken from the ruins of his once beautiful palace. When this was finished they tied the unhappy king in the midst of it, and one ran for a torch to set it on fire.

"Now we shall have a merry blaze," said the savage fellows. "What good can all his wealth do him now?"

As poor Croesus, bruised and bleeding, lay upon the pyre[4] without a friend to soothe his misery, he thought of the words that Solon had spoken to him years before: "No man can say whether you are happy or not until you die," and he moaned, "O Solon! O Solon! Solon!"

It so happened that Cyrus was riding by at that very moment and heard his moans. "What does he say?" he asked of the soldiers.

"He says, 'Solon, Solon, Solon!'" answered one.

Then the king rode nearer and asked Croesus, "Why do you call on the name of Solon?"

Croesus was silent at first. But after Cyrus had repeated his question kindly, he told all about Solon's visit at his palace and what he had said.

The story affected Cyrus deeply. He thought of the words, "No man knows what misfortunes may overtake you, or what misery may be yours in place of all this splendor." And he wondered if sometime he, too, would lose all his power and be helpless in the hands of his enemies.

"After all," said he, "ought not men to be merciful and kind to those who are in distress? I will do to Croesus as I would have others do to me." And he

3 Thereupon 그래서, 그런 까닭에
4 pyre 화장용 장작(더미)

caused Croesus to be given his freedom, and ever afterward treated him as one of his most honored friends.

—From *The Book of Virtucs* (pp. 135-37)

Grammatical Tips

● **비교**

영어의 비교급 사용에서 주의할 점은 비교 대상이 될 수 있도록 해야 한다.

즉, "Its vocabulary comes in part from Latin, while its grammar is similar to that of German."에서 '~과 비슷하다'는 similar to라는 비교 대상은 vocabulary이므로 'that (vocabulary) of'와 비교해야지 that of를 쓰지 않고 독일어와 비교하면 틀린 문장이 된다.

1. 동등비교

William is as poor as John (is poor).
= William's poverty is equal to John's.

2. 열등비교

Mary is less careful than Jane.
= Mary is not so (as) careful as Jane.

3. 우월비교

It is hotter today than it was yesterday.

*** 비교급 앞에 the를 쓰는 경우**

(1) Jim is the more stupid of the two boys.
(2) I like him all the better for his faults.
(비교급에 이유를 나타내는 구문이 뒤따르는 경우)
(3) The more a man has, the more he wants. (~하면 할수록 ~하다, 관용구)
(4) 막연히 구분하는 경우: the higher (lower) class

the younger generation
the greater part

4. 보통 발음되는 모음이 하나인 **단음절**에는 **-er, -est**로 비교급과 최상급을 나타낸다.

(1) 그러나 -er로 끝나는 2음절어: bitter, clever, tender (예외: eager, proper)
(2) -ow로 끝나는 2음절어: narrow, shallow, hollow, yellow
(3) -y로 끝나는 2음절어: pretty, heavy, easy, lazy, busy, angry, noisy, ugly, costly, holy
(4) -some으로 끝나는 2음절어: handsome, wholesome(건강에 좋은), winsome(애교 있는) (예외: irksome 지루한)
(5) -ture로 끝나는 2음절어: mature(성숙한)
(6) 일상적으로 쓰는 2음절어: cruel, pleasant, quiet, solid, common, civil, honest, stupid
(7) -e로 끝나는 2음절어: polite, secure, sincere, insane
(8) 3음절의 경우: unhappy, uncommon, bloodthirsty

5. 일반적으로 **2**음절어 이상은 **more, most**로 비교급과 최상급을 나타낸다.

(1) 그러나 서술적으로 쓰이는 다음절에는 more를 쓴다.:
kind, fond, real, right, just, like, wrong
No man is more kind and just than he.
I'm more fond of apples than pears.
(2) 동일인이나 동일한 사물의 성질을 비교할 때 단음절이더라도 more를 쓴다.
He is more(rather의 뜻) food than bad.
(3) 형용사+ly의 부사의 비교급은 more를 쓴다.
My brother eats more slowly than me.

6. 불규칙 비교

good(well) − better − best, bad(ill) − worse − worst
late − later − latest(시간), late − latter − last(순서)
up − upper − uppermost(upmost)
well-known − better-known − best-known
east(eastern) − easternmost, south(southern) − southmost

7. 최상급의 다른 형태

(1) as 형용사(부사) as ever 동사: He is as gentle as ever lived.

(2) as 형용사(부사) as any 명사: He is as gentle a man as any.

He is as gentle as any man.

(3) 비교급 than any other 단수명사: He is gentler than any other man.

(4) no (other) 주어+동사+ 비교급 than 주어: No other man is gentler than he.

(5) 부정주어+동사 so 형용사(부사) as 주어: No man is so gentle as he.

Nothing is so simple as this.

(6) 최상급이 주격보어로 사용될 때 the는 생략한다.: He is happiest now.

This river is deepest here.

(7) 최상급은 양보의 의미로도 쓰인다.: The wisest man can make a mistake.

(8) 비교급의 관용적 표현

I know better than to quarrel. (be not so foolish to ~할 만큼 어리석지 않다)

The temptation was more than I could bear. (~할 수 없다)

He was the last man (that) I expected to meet. (결코 ~하지 않을)

(9) 비교급이나 최상급을 만들 수 없는 형용사, 즉 절대적 의미를 가지는 형용사

perfect, unique, dead, principal, complete, wrong, total, main, right, well(건강한)

Exercise

A. Fill in the blanks with suitable word(s) or phrase(s).

1. A man's love of music does not depend ( ) education or social position.

2. A peasant can be as deeply moved by a great symphony ( ) a king.
   a. than b. more than c. less than d. as

3. Music ( ) an important role in society.
   a. gives b. give c. plays d. play

4. The armies of the world march ( ) music.
   a. in b. to c. with d. by

5. Just as music is a universal language, ( ) it is a mirror of the times.
   a. as b. so c. then d. than

6. There are still some people who refuse ( ) the value of jazz.
   a. to admit b. admitting c. admitted d. to be admitted

B. Match the following words with their similar and opposite meanings. Write the correct letters on the lines.

Similar Meaning

1. ___ famous	a. hurricane
2. ___ powerful	b. lost
3. ___ cause	c. strong
4. ___ murderer	d. unfortunate
5. ___ storm	e. well-known
6. ___ poor	f. killer
7. ___ confused	g. reason

Opposite Meaning

1. ___ alive	a. terrible
2. ___ content	b. unhappy
3. ___ loud	c. calm
4. ___ upset	d. poor
5. ___ wonderful	e. stand up
6. ___ rich	f. dead
7. ___ lie down	g. quiet

C. Explain the underlined.

1. You make me <u>of no account</u>.

2. No man knows what misfortunes may <u>overtake</u> you, or what misery may be yours <u>in place of all this splendor</u>.

D. Answer the questions.

1. What may be the common thematic(key) word in the above two essays?
   a. Harmony b. Difference c. Direction d. Pleasure

2. Cyrus said, "I will do to Croesus as I would have others do to me."
   Which is not similar to the underlined?
   a. Do as you would be done by. (남이 당신에게 해주기 원하는 대로 남에게 하라.)
   b. What you dislike for yourself do not like for me.
   c. Expect to be treated as you have treated others.
   d. Do to others as you would have them do to you. (대접받으려면 대접해라.)
   e. Do for others what you want them to do for you.
   (다른 사람이 해주기 바라는 대로 다른 사람들에게 하라.)
   f. The more noble, the more humble. (고상할수록 겸손하다.)

Unit 9

9-1. *The Tower of Babel*

9-2. *The Golden Touch*

9-1.

The Tower of Babel

The story of the Tower of Babel appears in the Old Testament. In an attempt to understand the mysteries of God, men tried to build a tower that would reach to heaven. As a punishment for their pride, the tower collapsed and the language of the workers became confused. This is an allegorical explanation of the origin of the various languages that are spoken throughout the world. Today more than one thousand languages are spoken. Many of them stem from a common source. The Romance Languages—such as French, Spanish, and Italian—are all derived from Latin. English, on the other hand, has borrowed elements from many languages. Its vocabulary comes in part from Latin, while its grammar is similar to that of German.

In the Middle Ages, Latin was the universal language.[1] Most university classes were conducted in Latin, and all important documents were written in that language. Gradually, however, Latin fell into disuse, and by the eighteenth century, French had become the language of diplomacy. Today, however,

---

1 the universal language 세계어, 공용어

English is commonly used to transact[2] international affairs. For this reason, English is referred to as a universal language. It is becoming increasingly important as a means of overcoming the language barriers that exist between the various countries of the world. It can truly be said that the man who speaks English possesses an important tool for communicating with other people throughout the world.

There are various reasons why English has come to occupy the important position it does today. The few dialects in English give it the advantage of being a standard language. In addition, English is very exact. It has few of the ambiguities[3] that are found in many other modern tongues. This makes it ideal for the transaction of business and international affairs. The biggest drawback[4] to English as a universal language, however, is its difficult pronunciation. In addition, the many exceptions to the rules of English usage make it difficult to master. However, the satisfaction of being able to speak this widely used language makes the study of English well worthwhile.

Language is one of man's most precious possessions. Without it, he would be unable to exchange ideas with his fellow men. In the modern world, however, it is not enough to speak only the language of one's own country. It is said that the man who speaks two languages has two minds, for in learning a foreign language, we acquire, to a certain extent[5], the mentality[6] of a foreign people. Language study, accordingly, is one of the best means of enabling us to understand our fellow men. It is difficult, to be sure, but rich in rewards. It

2 transact 처리하다 cf. transaction 거래
3 ambiguities 애매함
4 drawback 결점, 약점
5 to a certain extent 어느 정도
6 the mentality: way of thinking

makes us better citizens of the international world in which we live.

Dream

We must never stop dreaming. Dreams provide nourishment[7] for the soul, just as a meal does for the body. Many times in our lives we see our dreams shattered[8] and our desires frustrated, but we have to continue dreaming. If we don't, our soul dies, and agape[9] cannot reach it.

The good fight is the one that's fought in the name of our dreams. When we're young and our dreams first explode inside us with all of their force, we are very courageous, but we haven't yet learned how to fight. With great effort, we learn how to fight, but by then we no longer have the courage to go into combat. So we turn against ourselves and do battle within. We become our own worst enemy. We say that our dreams were childish, or too difficult to realize, or the result of our not having known enough about life. We kill our dreams because we are afraid to fight the good fight.

The first symptom of the process of our killing our dreams is the lack of time. The busiest people always have time enough to do everything. Those who do nothing are always tired and pay no attention to the little amount of work they are required to do. They complain constantly that the day is too short. The truth is, they are afraid to fight the good fight.

—Adapted from Paulo Coelho (pp. 56-58)

---

7 nourishment: something that nourishes; food: the child took no nourishment all day.

8 shattered: 1. broken suddenly into very small pieces, usually as a result of force or violence: I dropped the mirror on the floor and it shattered. Hopes of reaching an agreement were shattered today. 2. shock; have a strong effect on the feelings of: We were shattered to hear of her sudden death.

9 agape[a:gá:pei] 사랑, 아가페(비타산적 사랑)

Exercise

* Answer the questions.

1. What is the biggest drawback to English as a universal language?
   a. Its vocabulary   b. Its pronunciation   c. Its grammar   d. Its alphabet

2. What could be the good fight for us?
   a. one that's fought in the name of our dreams
   b. one that's fought in the name of God
   c. one that's fought in the name of our ideologies
   d. one that's fought in the name of our knowledge

* Find the opposite meaning to the underlined.

1. The few <u>dialects</u> in English give it the advantage of being a standard language.

2. We acquire the mentality of a <u>foreign</u> people.

3. Language is one of man's most <u>precious</u> possessions.

9-2.

The Golden Touch

This retelling of the famous Greek tale about lust for gold is adapted from Nathaniel Hawthorne's version in his *Wonder Book*. The Midas of mythology is usually identified by scholars with a king of ancient Phrygia (now Turkey) who ruled in the eighth century B.C. The early Greeks believed Phrygia to be a land of fabulous wealth.

Once upon a time there lived a very rich king whose name was Midas. He had more gold than anyone in the whole world, but for all that,[1] he thought it was not enough. He was never so happy as when he happened to get more gold to add to his treasure. He stored it away in great vaults[2] underneath his palace, and many hours of each day were spent counting it over.

Now King Midas had a little daughter named Marygold. He loved her devotedly, and said: "She shall be the richest princess in all the world!"

But little Marygold cared nothing about it all. She loved her garden, her flowers and the golden sunshine more than all her father's riches. She was a

---

1 for all that 그렇게 많은 금을 가지고 있음에도 불구하고
2 vault[vɔːlt] 지하실, 금고실

lonely little girl most of the time, for her father was so busy planning new ways to get more gold, and counting what he had, that he seldom told her stories or went for walks with her, as all fathers should do.

One day King Midas was down in his treasure room. He had locked the heavy doors and had opened up his great chests of gold. He piled it on the table and handled it as if he loved the touch of it. He let it slip through his fingers and smiled at the clink of it as if it had been sweet music. Suddenly a shadow fell over the heap of gold. Looking up, he saw a stranger dressed in shining white smiling down at him. King Midas started up in surprise. Surely he had not failed to lock the door! His treasure was not safe! But the stranger continued to smile.

"You have much gold, King Midas," he said.

"Yes," said the king, "but think how little this is to all the gold there is in the world!"

"What! Are you not satisfied?" asked the stranger.

"Satisfied?" said the king. "Of course I'm not. I often lie awake through the long night planning new ways to get more gold. I wish that everything I touch would turn to gold."

"Do you really wish that, King Midas?"

"Of course I wish it. Nothing could make me so happy."

"Then you shall have your wish. Tomorrow morning when the first rays of the sun fall through your window you shall have the golden touch."

When he had finished speaking, the stranger vanished. King Midas rubbed his eyes. "I must have dreamed it," he said, "but how happy I should be if it were only true!"

The next morning King Midas woke when the first faint light came into his room. He put out his hand and touched the covers of his bed. Nothing happened. "I knew it could not be true," he sighed. Just at that moment the first rays of the sun came through the window. The covers on which King Midas's hand lay became pure gold. "It's true, it's true!" he cried joyfully.

He sprang out of bed and ran about the room touching everything. His dressing gown, his slippers, the furniture, all became gold. He looked out of the window through Marygold's garden.

"I'll give her a nice surprise," he said. He went down into the garden touching all of Marygold's flowers, and changing them to gold. "She will be so pleased," he thought.

He went back into his room to wait for his breakfast; and took up his book which he had been reading the night before, but the minute he touched it, it was solid gold. "I can't read it now," he said, "but of course it is far better to have it gold."

Just then a servant came through the door with the king's breakfast. "How good it looks," he said. "I'll have that ripe, red peach first of all."

He took the peach in his hand, but before he could taste it, it became a lump of gold. King Midas put it back on the plate. "It's very beautiful, but I can't eat it!" he said. He took a roll from the plate, but that, too, became gold. "What shall I do?" he cried. "I am hungry and thirsty, I can't eat or drink gold!"

At that moment the door was opened and in came little Marygold. She was crying bitterly, and in her hand was one of her roses.

"What's the matter, little daughter?" said the king.

"Oh, Father! See what has happened to all my roses! They are stiff, ugly things!"

"Why, they are golden roses, child. Do you not think they are more beautiful than they were?"

"No," she sobbed, "they do not smell sweet. They won't grow anymore. I like roses that are alive."

"Never mind," said the king, "eat your breakfast now."

But Marygold noticed that her father did not eat, and that he looked very sad. "What is the matter, Father dear?" she said, and she ran over to him. She threw her arms about him, and he kissed her. But he suddenly cried out in terror and anguish. When he touched her, her lovely little face became glittering gold, her eyes could not see, her lips could not kiss him back again, her little arms could not hold him close. She was no longer a loving, laughing little girl; she was changed to a little golden statue.

King Midas bowed his head and great sobs shook him.

"Are you happy, King Midas?" he heard a voice say. Looking up he saw the stranger standing near him.

"Happy! How can you ask? I am the most miserable man living!" said the king.

"You have the golden touch," said the stranger. "Is that not enough?"

King Midas did not look up or answer.

"Which would you rather have, food and a cup of cold water or these lumps of gold?" said the stranger.

King Midas could not answer.

"Which would you rather have, O King—that little golden statue, or a little girl who could run, and laugh, and love you?"

"Oh, give me back my little Marygold and I'll give up all the gold I have!" said the king. "I've lost all that was worth having."

"You are wiser than you were, King Midas," said the stranger. "Go plunge in the river which runs at the foot of your garden, then take some of its water and sprinkle whatever you wish to change back as it was." The stranger vanished.

King Midas sprang up and ran to the river. He plunged into it, and then he dipped up a pitcher of its water and hurried back to the palace. He sprinkled it over Marygold, and the color came back into her cheeks. She opened her blue eyes again. "Why, Father!" she said. "What happened?"

With a cry of joy King Midas took her into his arms.

Never after that did King Midas care for any gold except the gold of sunshine, and the gold of little Marygold's hair.

—From *The Book of Virtues* (pp. 63-66)

Grammatical Tips

● **수동태**(Passive Voice)

목적어가 있는 3형식에서 5형식까지 수동태가 가능하다. 수동태의 문장은 능동태보다 그 내용을 완곡하게 표현할 수 있다. 능동태를 수동태로 바꾸는 방식은 다음과 같다.

1. 3형식: 주어+타동사+목적어 →
   주어(능동태 목적어)+be 과거분사 by(with) 목적어(능동태 주어)

   Private individuals cannot do this.
   → This cannot be done by private individuals.

2. 4형식: 주어+타동사+간접목적어+직접목적어 →
   주어(간접목적어 또는 직접목적어) be 과거분사 직접목적어 또는 간접목적어+목적어(능동태 주어)

   He bought her a new hat.
   → A new hat was bought (for) her by him.

   * 다음 동사들은 직접목적어만 수동태의 주어로 한다.
   buy, make, sell, afford, carry, ensure, get, hand, intend, mean, pass, read, reach, write, yield

   * 간접목적어만 수동태의 주어로 하는 동사들은 다음과 같다.
   strike, envy, ask, spare, save, call

3. 부정사를 쓰는 수동태는 의욕, 요구, 허락, 금지를 나타내는 동사들이다.

want, expect, advise, persuade, urge, like, encourage, require, request, ask, forbid, allow, prohibit, disallow

We forced him to sign the paper.

→ He was forced to sign the paper.

4. by 이외의 전치사를 사용하는 경우

(1) be 희노애락 at: pleased, delighted, grieved, surprised, angered, enraged, amazed

(2) be (불)만족, 재료 with: satisfied, dissatisfied, pleased, troubled, covered, topped

(3) be 실망, 흥미, 종사 in: interested, absorbed, disappointed, engaged, employed, involved

(4) be 방향 to: married, known, unknown, accustomed, adjusted, devoted, exposed

(5) be 원료 from: made from, brewed from

(6) be 재료 of: built of, composed of

(7) be 변화 into: changed, made, persuaded

Exercise

* Make each sentence using the following idiom or word(s).

1. confuse

2. derive from

3. on the one hand, on the other hand

4. dialect, standard language

5. (1) transact, transaction
   (2) transport, transportation
   (3) transform, transformation
   (4) transplant, transplantation

6. refer to

7. to some extent

8. world citizen, citified man

* Who is the first citified man? See "Genesis" in Old Testament.

* Discuss the following words.

dream, hope, challenge, adventure

Unit 10

10-1. *The Blanket*

10-2. *Responsibility*

10-1.

The Blanket

—Floyd Dell[1]

It was a fine September night, with a silver moon riding high over the gully.[2] Petey, eleven years old, did not see the moon. He did not feel the cool September breeze blow into the kitchen, for his thoughts were fixed on a red and black blanket on the kitchen table.

The blanket was gift from his Dad to his Granddad ... a going-away gift. They said that Granddad was going away ... that's what they call it "going away."

Petey hadn't really believed that Dad would be doing it—sending Granddad away. "Away" was what they were calling it. Not until now could he believe it of Dad.[3]

---

1 Dell was born in Barry, Illinois on June 28, 1887. As a literary critic, Dell had a national reputation for promoting modern American literature in the 1910s. He was a best-selling author of novels and books of stories and essays, as well as a lifelong poet and the author of a hit Broadway play, *Little Accident* (1928). His influence is alive in the work of many major American writers from the first half of the 20th century.

2 gully: valley

3 Not until now could he believe it of Dad. 부정어나 부사로 시작되면 의문문이 아닌 평서문이라도 도치, 즉 동사+주어의 어순이 된다. 원래 어순은 He could not believe it of Dad until now.

But here was the blanket that Dad had that day bought for him, and in the morning he'd be going away. And this was the last evening they'd be having together. Dad was off seeing[4] that girl he was to marry. He'd not be back till late, and they could sit up and talk.

When they'd washed up the supper dishes, they went out on the shanty porch,[5] the old man and the boy, taking their chairs. "I'll get me fiddle,"[6] said the old man, "and play you some of the old tunes." But instead of the fiddle he brought out the blanket. It was a big, double blanket, red, with black cross stripes.

"Now, isn't that a fine blanket?" said the old man, smoothing it over his knees. "And isn't it your father a kind man to be giving the old fellow a blanket like that to go away with? It cost something, it did—look at the wool of it! And warm it will be these cold winter nights to come. There'll be few blankets there equal to this one!"

It was like Granddad to be saying that. He was trying to make it easier. He'd pretended all along it was he that was wanting to away to the great brick building—the government place, where he'd be with so many other old fellows having the best of everything ... but Petey hadn't believed Dad would really do it, until this night when he brought home the blanket.

"Oh, yes it's a fine blanket," said Petey, and got up and went into the shanty. He wasn't the kind to cry, and besides, he was too old for that, being eleven. He'd just come in to fetch[7] Granddad's fiddle.

---

4 see off 배웅하다
5 shanty porch 오두막 입구(현관)
6 fiddle: violin
7 fetch 가져오다

The blanket slid[8] to the floor as the old man took the fiddle and stood up. It was the last night they'd be having together. There wasn't any need to say, "Play all the old tunes." Granddad tuned up for a minute, and then said, "This one you'll like to remember."

The silver moon was high overhead, and there was a gentle breeze[9] playing down the gully. He'd never be hearing Granddad play like this again. It was as well Dad was moving into that new house, away from here. He'd not want, Petey wouldn't, to sit here on the old porch of fine evenings, with Granddad gone.

The tune changed. "Here's something gayer."[10] Petey sat and stared out over the gully. Dad would marry that girl. Yes, that girl who'd kissed him and slobbered over[11] him, saying she'd try to be a good mother to him, and all ... His chair creaked[12] as he involuntarily[13] gave his body a painful twist.

The tune stopped suddenly, and Granddad said: "It's a poor tune, except to be dancing to."[14] And then: "It's a fine girl your father's going to marry. He'll be feeling young again, with a pretty wife like that. And what would an old fellow like me be doing around their house, getting in the way,[15] an old nuisance,[16] what with my talk of aches and pains! And then there'll be babies coming, and I'd not want to be there to hear them crying at all hours. It's best that I take myself off, like I'm doing. One more tune or two, and then we'll be

---

8 slide-slid-slid
9 breeze 미풍
10 gay: fun
11 slobbered over: fell in love with
12 creaked 삐걱거리다
13 involuntarily 모르는 사이에
14 except to be dancing to [the tune] 그 곡조에 맞춰 춤추는 것 말고는
15 getting in the way 방해가 되면서
16 nuisance[nju:səns] 골칫덩이, 성가심

going to bed to get some sleep against the morning, when I'll pack up my fine blanket and take my leave. Listen to this, will you? It's a bit sad, but a fine tune for a night like this."

They didn't hear the two people coming down the gully path, Dad and the pretty girl with the hard, bright face like a china doll's. But they heard her laugh, right by the porch, and the tune stopped on a wrong, high, startled note. Dad didn't say anything, but the girl came forward and spoke to Granddad prettily: "I'll not be seeing you leave in the morning, so I came over to say good-bye."

"It's kind of you,"[17] said Granddad, with his eyes cast down; and then, seeing the blanket at his feet, he stopped to pick it up. "And will you look at this," he said in embarrassment, "the fine blanket my son has given me to go away with!"

"Yes," she said, "it's a fine blanket." She felt of the wool, and repeated in surprise, "A fine blanket—I'll say it is!" She turned to Dad, and said to him coldly, "It cost something, that."

He cleared his throat,[18] and said defensively, "I wanted him to have the best ..."

The girl stood there, still intent on the blanket. "It's double, too," she said reproachfully to Dad.

"Yes," said Granddad, "it's double—a fine blanket for an old fellow to be going away with."

The boy went abruptly[19] into the shanty. He was looking for something.

---

17 사람의 감정을 나타내는 형용사들은 of를 동반한다. considerate of 등.

18 cleared his throat (목소리를 가다듬기 위해) 헛기침을 하다

19 abruptly: suddenly

He could hear that girl reproaching Dad, and Dad becoming angry in his slow way. And now she was suddenly going away in a huff[20] ... As Petey came out, she turned and called back, "All the same, he doesn't need a double blanket!" And she ran up the gully path.

Dad was looking after her uncertainly.

"Oh, she's right," said the boy coldly. "Here, Dad"—and he held out a pair of scissors. "Cut the blanket in two."

Both of them stared at the boy, startled. "Cut it in two, I tell you, Dad!" he cried out. "And keep the other half!"

"That's not a bad idea," said Granddad gently. "I don't need so much of a blanket."

"Yes," said the boy harshly, "a single blanket's enough for an old man when he's sent away. We'll save the other half, Dad; it will come in handy[21] later."

"Now, what do you mean by that?" asked Dad.

"I mean," said the boy slowly, "that I'll give it to you, Dad—when you're old and I'm sending you—away."

There was a silence, and then Dad went over to Granddad and stood before him, not speaking. But Granddad understood, for he put out a hand and laid it on Dad's shoulder. Petey was watching them. And he heard Granddad whisper, "It's all right, son—I knew you didn't mean it..." And then Petey cried.

But it didn't matter—because they were all three crying together.

—Adapted

---

20 in a huff 불끈해서

21 come in handy 소용이 되는, 편리한

Excercise

1. Which one would be the government place in the passage, if we say it in other way?
   a. hospital b. clinic c. kindergarten d. nursing home

2. What response would be Petey and Granddad on Dad's remarriage?
   a. positive b. reluctant c. thoughtful d. considerate

3. What is the predominant symbol in this tale?
   a. fiddle b. blanket c. china doll d. moon e. scissors

4. What is the author saying about old age and the difference between generations?
   a. There really is an enormous difference between the three generations.
   b. Old age is golden time.
   c. It is better to be young than old.
   d. There is no real "generation gap": we will all be old someday.

5. What is the overall tone of this story?
   a. melancholic b. cheerful c. uplifting d. sarcastic

6. The term "china doll" was selected to describe the girl because
   a. she is very pretty and uses cosmetics to the best advantage.
   b. her "hard, bright face" reveals her true nature.
   c. it explains why Petey and Granddad admire her.
   d. she has very fine manners, revealed when she says goodbye to Granddad.

7. The word "shanty" suggests
   a. a broad, expansive country estate.
   b. a well-to-do family.
   c. an historic old home.
   d. miserable poverty.

8. The "scissors" best represent

a. severing the bonds of love, (filial) duty, respect.

b. severing the bonds of unpleasant duty.

c. cutting loose from that which is holding you back.

d. assuming new freedoms and human possibility.

* apostrophe d('d)의 두 가지 용례를 본문에서 찾아 각각 무엇의 줄임 꼴인지 밝히시오.

10-2.

Responsibility

To "respond" is to "answer." Correspondingly, to be "responsible" is to be "answerable," to be *accountable.* Irresponsible behavior is immature behavior. Taking responsibility—being responsible—is a sign of maturity. When we strive to help our children become responsible persons, we are helping them toward maturity. James Madison delimited the parameters of responsibility with characteristic clarity in *Federalist* No. 63. "Responsibility, in order to be reasonable, must be limited to objects within the power of the responsible party, and in order to be effectual, must relate to operations of that power." Persons who have not reached maturity have not yet come into full ownership of their powers.

It is a truism that everything which has ever been *done* in the history of the world has been done *by somebody*; some person has exercised some power to *do* it. Our share of the responsibility for what we do individually or in concert with others varies with the social and political structures within which we operate, but it characteristically increases with maturity. It was an immature Adam in the Garden of Eden who, when discovered to have eaten of the forbidden fruit, laid it on the beguiling serpent.[1] "She made me do it"/"He made me do it" is an archetypal drama reenacted in every generation where siblings[2] and playmates are called upon to answer for their misdoings.

But it doesn't stop there. An unwitting acknowledgement of this sort of immaturity commonly continues on into adulthood. Nearly everyone has an excuse when things go wrong. In Washington, D.C., common parlance[3] makes ample use of the passive voice to avoid blame: "mistakes were made." But there is no rush to take responsibility. There is no shortage of persons ready to claim credit for contributing to an enterprise that goes well, however, even though a maxim familiar to persons in public service observes that "There is no end to the good you can do if you don't care who gets credit for it."[4]

In the end, we are answerable for the kinds of persons we have made of ourselves. "That's just the way I am!" is not an excuse for inconsiderate or vile behavior.[5] Nor is it even an accurate description, for we are never *just* what we are. As Aristotle was among the first to insist, we *become* what we are as persons by the decisions that we ourselves make. British philosopher Mary Midgley points out in *Beast and Man* that "the really excellent and central point of Existentialism [is] the acceptance of responsibility for being as we have made ourselves, the refusal to make bogus[6] excuses."

Søren Kierkegaard, one of Existentialism's nineteenth-century pioneers, deplored the damaging effects of crowds and gangs on our *sense* of

1 laid it on the beguiling serpent 그것(금지한 과일을 먹은 행위)을 기만한 뱀의 탓으로 돌렸다(전가했다)
2 siblings 형제자매
3 common parlance 일반적 말투
4 gets credit for it 그것(선한 일)의 공로를 인정받다
5 an excuse for inconsiderate or vile behavior 지각(분별)없거나 비열한 행위에 대한 변명
6 bogus 가짜의; 믿을 수 없는

responsibility. "A crowd," as he wrote in *The Point of View for My Work as an Author*, "in its very concept is the untruth, by reason of the fact that it renders the individual completely impenitent and irresponsible, or at least weakens his sense of responsibility by reducing it to a fraction."[7] In his *Confessions* St. Augustine made this weakened sense of responsibility under peer pressure a central feature of his meditation upon the vandalism of his youth,[8] "all because we are ashamed to hold back[9] when others say 'Come on! Let's do it!'" But he was as insistent as Aristotle and the Existentialists on recognizing personal responsibility for what he had done. A weakened *sense* of responsibility does not weaken the *fact* of responsibility.

Responsible persons are mature people who have taken charge of themselves and their conduct, who *own* their actions and *own up to* them[10]—who *answer* for them. We help foster a mature sense of responsibility in our children in the same way that we help cultivate their other desirable traits: by practice and by example. Household chores, homework, extracurricular activities, after-school jobs, and volunteer work all contribute to maturation if parental example and expectations are clear, consistent, and commensurate wit h[11] the developing powers of the child.

—From *The Book of Virtue* (pp. 185-86)

---

7 "A crowd," "in its very concept is the untruth, by reason of the fact that it renders the individual completely impenitent and irresponsible, or at least weakens his sense of responsibility by reducing it to a fraction." "하나의 집단"이란 그 개념상 오류다. 그 개념이 온전히 회개하지 않고 책임 없는 개인이 되게 하거나 적어도 그 개념을 파편으로 축소시켜 개인의 책임의식을 약화시킨다는 사실 때문이다. cf. impenitent[impenətənt] 회개하지 않는, 완고한, fraction 파편, 단편

8 St. Augustine made this weakened sense of responsibility under peer pressure a central feature of his meditation upon the vandalism of his youth 성 오거스틴은 이렇게 약화된 책임감을 자신이 젊었을 때의 만행에 대해 같은 압박감을 느끼며 자기 묵상의 중심으로 삼았다.

9 hold back 말리다; 억제, 자제시키다

10 *own* their actions and *own up to* them 자기들의 행위라고 하고 그 행위들을 인정하는

11 commensurate[kəmenʃərit] with 걸맞은, 상응한

Unit 11

11-1. *King Alfred and the Cakes*

11-2. *The Sword of Damocles*

11-3. *Food*

11-1.

King Alfred and the Cakes

Alfred the Great was king of the West Saxons in England during the ninth century. His determination to protect England from Danish conquest and his emphasis on literacy and education for his people have lifted him into the ranks of England's most popular rulers. This famous story reminds us that attention to little duties prepares us to meet larger ones. It also reminds us that leadership and responsibility walk hand in hand and that truly great leaders do not disdain small responsibilities.

In England many years ago there ruled a king named Alfred. A wise and just man, Alfred was one of the best kings England ever had. Even today, centuries later, he is known as Alfred the Great.

The days of Alfred's rule were not easy ones in England. The country was invaded by the fierce Danes, who had come from across the sea. There were so many Danish invaders, and they were so strong and bold, that for a long time they won almost every battle. If they kept on winning, they would soon be masters of the whole country.

At last, after so many struggles, King Alfred's English army was broken and scattered. Every man had to save himself in the best way he could, including King Alfred. He disguised himself as a shepherd and fled alone through the woods and swamps.

After several days of wandering, he came to the hut of a woodcutter. Tired and hungry, he knocked on the door and begged the woodcutter's wife to give him something to eat and a place to sleep.

The woman looked with pity at the ragged fellow. She had no idea who he really was. "Come in," she said. "I will give you some supper if you will watch these cakes I am baking on the hearth. I want to go out and milk the cow. Watch them carefully, and make sure they don't burn while I'm gone."

Alfred thanked her politely and sat down beside the fire. He tried to pay attention to the cakes, but soon all his troubles filled his mind. How was he going to get his army together again? And even if he did, how was he going to prepare it to face the Danes? How could he possibly drive such fierce invaders out of England? The more he thought, the more hopeless the future seemed, and he began to believe there was no use in continuing to fight. Alfred saw only his problems. He forgot he was in the woodcutter's hut, he forgot about his hunger, and he forgot all about the cakes.

In a little while, the woman came back. She found her hut full of smoke and her cakes burned to a crisp. And there was Alfred sitting beside the hearth, gazing into the flames. He had never even noticed the cakes were burning.

"You lazy, good-for-nothing fellow!" the woman cried. "Look what you've done! You want something to eat, but you don't want to work for it! Now none of us will have any supper!" Alfred only hung his head[1] in shame.

Just then the woodcutter came home. As soon as he walked through the

1 hung(hid) his head 고개를 숙이다

door, he recognized the stranger sitting at his hearth.

"Be quiet!" he told his wife. "Do you realize who you are scolding? This is our noble ruler, King Alfred himself."

The woman was horrified. She ran to the king's side fell to her knees. She begged him to forgive her for speaking so harshly.

But the wise King Alfred asked her to rise. "You were right to scold me," he said. "I told you I would watch the cakes, and then I let them burn. I deserved what you said. Anyone who accepts a duty, whether it be large or small, should perform it faithfully. I have failed this time, but it will not happen again. My duties as king await me."

The story does not tell us if King Alfred had anything to eat that night. But it was not many days before he had gathered his men together again, and soon he drove the Danes out of England.

—From *The Book of Virtues* (pp. 197–98)

Exercise

A. Match the opposite one.

1. ____ literacy	a. timid
2. ____ disdain	b. respect
3. ____ just	c. illiteracy
4. ____ bold	d. wrong
5. ____ scatter	e. smoothly
6. ____ harshly	f. gather

B. Correct the underlined.

1. He disguised himself as a shepherd and <u>flees</u> alone through the woods and swamps.

2. <u>Tiring</u> and hungry, he knocked on the door and begged the woodcutter's wife to give him something to eat and a place to sleep.

3. My duties as king <u>awaits</u> me.

4. It was not many days before he had gathered his men together again, and soon he <u>drives</u> the Danes out of England.

11-2.

The Sword of Damocles

This is one of our oldest "if you can't stand the heat, get out of the kitchen" stories. It is a great reminder that if we aspire to any kind of high office or job, we must be willing to live with all the burdens that come with it.

There once was a king named Dionysius who ruled in Syracuse, the richest city in Sicily. He lived in a fine palace where there were many beautiful and costly things, and he was waited upon by a host of servants who were always ready to do his bidding.

Naturally, because Dionysius had so much wealth and power, there were many in Syracuse who envied his good fortune. Damocles[1] was one of these. He was one of Dionysius's best friends, and he was always saying to him, "How lucky you are! You have everything anyone could wish for. You must be the happiest man in the world."

One day Dionysius grew tired of hearing such talk. "Come now," he said,

---

1 Damocles[dǽməkliːz] (그리스 신화) Syracuse의 왕 Dionysius의 신하. *the sword of Damocles* = *Damocles' sword* 신변에 따라다니는 위험(Dionysius 왕이 연석에서 Damocles 머리 위에 머리카락 하나로 칼을 매달아, 왕위에 따르는 위험을 보여준 일에서)

"do you really think I'm happier than everyone else?"

"But of course you are," Damocles replied. "Look at the great treasures you possess, and the power you hold. You have not a single worry in the world. How could life be any better?"

"Perhaps you would like to change places with me," said Dionysius.

"Oh, I would never dream of that," said Damocles. "But if I could only have your riches and your pleasures for one day, I should never want any greater happiness."

"Very well. Trade places with me for just one day, and you shall have them."

And so, the next day, Damocles was led to the palace, and all the servants were instructed to treat him as their master. They dressed him in royal robes, and placed on his head a crown of gold. He sat down at a table in the banquet hall, and rich foods were set before him. Nothing was wanting that could give him pleasure. There were costly wines, and beautiful flowers, and rare perfumes, and delightful music. He rested himself among soft cushions, and felt he was the happiest man in all the world.

"Ah, this is the life," he sighed to Dionysius, who sat at the other end of the long table. "I've never enjoyed myself so much."

And as he raised a cup to his lips, he lifted his eyes toward the ceiling. What was that dangling above him, with its point almost touching his head?

Damocles stiffened. The smile faded from his lips, and his face turned ashy pale. His hands trembled. He wanted to be no more food, no more wine, no more music. He only wanted to be out of the palace, far away, he cared not where. For directly above his head hung a sword, held to the ceiling by only a single horsehair. Its sharp blade glittered as it pointed right between his eyes.

He started to jump up and run, but stopped himself, frightened that any sudden move might snap the thin thread and bring the sword down. He sat frozen to his chair.

"What is the matter, my friend?" Dionysius asked. "You seem to have lost your appetite."

"That sword! That sword!" whispered Damocles. "Don't you see it?"

"Of course I see it," said Dionysius. "I see it every day. It always hang over my head, and there is always the chance someone or something may cut the slim thread. Perhaps one of my own advisors will grow jealous of my power and try to kill me. Or someone may spread lies about me, to turn the people against me. It may be that a neighboring kingdom will send an army to seize this throne. Or I might make an unwise decision that will bring my downfall. If you want to be a leader, you must be willing to accept these risks. They come with the power, you see."

"Yes, I do see," said Damocles. "I see now that I was mistaken, and that you have much to think about besides your riches and fame. Please take your place, and let me go back to my own house."

And as long as he lived, Damocles never again wanted to change places, even for a moment, with the king.

—From *The Book of Virtues* (pp. 213–15)

Exercise

* Choose the similar expression to the given one.

1. "If you can't stand the heat, get out of the kitchen."
   a. Take it or leave it.
   b. When the wolf grows old, the crows ride him.
   c. There is no rule that has no exception.
   d. Do in Rome as the Romans do.

2. If we aspire to any kind of high office or job, we must be willing to live with all the burdens that come with it.
   a. High place, great danger.
   b. Manners makes man.
   c. Give and take.
   d. Don't open a shop unless you know how to smile.

* Choose the closest meaning to the underlined.

1. Dionysius <u>grew</u> tired of hearing such talk.
   a. was　　b. became　　c. put　　d. set

2. "<u>Trade</u> places with me for just one day."
   a. Sell　　b. Set　　c. Exchange　　d. Provide

3. The smile <u>faded</u> from his lips.
   a. appeared　　b. lingered　　c. sprang　　d. disappeared

4. You must be willing to accept these <u>risks</u>.

a. appetizers　　b. worries　　c. burdens　　d. dangers

5. He was waited upon by <u>a host of</u> servants who were always ready to do his <u>bidding</u>.

a. lots of–begging　　b. a lot of–ordering

c. a guest of–commanding　　d. a group of–begging

11-3.

Food

Food for all is the crucial[1] problem of the world today for several reasons. A hungry world is never likely to be a peaceful world. It is not saying too much to suggest that unrest throughout the world most frequently has its root cause in dissatisfaction with that part of the standard of living concerned with food. As Le Gros Clark has put it, a stable[2] civilization will be built only on the foundations of the farm and the kitchen.

We do well to remind ourselves that we consume food for three reasons. A large part of the food we eat keeps us going and provides the body with its heat and energy. It has precisely the same function as fuel performs with our modern machinery. However perfect the machine, it will not function[3] without the right fuel in adequate[4] quantities. Vaguely this idea has been apparent to man for a long time. Our ancestors used to talk about a man's strength failing

---

1 crucial: decisive, important
2 stable: firmly established
3 function(v): to operate, to work
4 adequate: sufficient, competent (opp. inadequate)

through lack of food. If for a short time the intake[5] of this fuel is inadequate, the body is able to call upon reserves[6] normally stored in the tissues,[7] but ultimately this stored material is used up and starvation results. For the fuel purpose of food we are concerned particularly with carbohydrates[8]—our daily bread.

In the second place, we consume food for building up the machine itself, that is to say for the development of the body. It is for this purpose that we require particularly the complex substances known as proteins, builders of muscles and other tissues. We have come to realize in recent years the important part played also by those essential substances to which the term vitamin is applied. They are diverse[9] in chemical composition and in function, and they are only required in small quantities; yet they are fundamental in the body's economy,[10] and the body itself cannot manufacture them from simple raw materials. In rather the same way certain chemical elements are necessary in small quantities—calcium for bone, minute quantities of iodine[11] for teeth, small quantities of iron for healthy red blood, and so on.

Thirdly, we consume food for what perhaps may be called its psychological effect. In these days the art of gracious living,[12] to which our ancestors were perhaps too much addicted,[13] has been almost forgotten, but probably all of us appreciate[14] that a tastefully served and well-balanced meal,

---

5 intake: that which is taken in 흡입
6 reserves 보유물, 보존물
7 tissues: a mass of similar cells
8 carbohydrate: a compound of carbon, hydrogen, and oxygen
9 diverse: several, sundry
10 economy 조직
11 iodine 요오드, 옥소
12 gracious living: living as a cultured person should
13 addicted: enslaved to a habit
14 appreciate: to estimate highly

eaten in pleasant surroundings, gives us a greater satisfaction than the same mixture of carbohydrates, proteins, and vitamins consumed from a tin mug on the floor. A graphic illustration is afforded by a recent experiment carried out in a British hospital. Groups of people were served with first-class food–good meat and well-cooked potatoes, but the meat was coloured green and the potatoes magenta[15] and other fierce colours. The majority of the 'guinea pigs'[16] were so affected psychologically that they were ill after eating the completely innocuous[17] meal.

In the long view a monotonous diet,[18] even if pronounced adequate, will not necessarily maintain the full vigour[19] of either individual or nation, however satisfactory it may be during stress,[20] as in wartime. The widely held view that many people live on an extremely monotonous diet and like it–one thinks of the boiled rice, occasionally flavoured with a little fat pork, and the weak tea of the Chinese–is far from the truth. Given the opportunity and the means, all peoples turn to a varied diet.

–L. Dudley Stamp: *Our Undeveloped World,*
from A University Anthology for Overseas Students (pp. 137–39)

---

15 magenta[mədʒentə]: a reddish purple
16 guinea pig: a kind of rodent often used for biological experiments
17 innocuous: harmless
18 diet: planned selection of food
19 vigour, vigor: 활력, 힘
20 stress(n): hardship, strain

Exercise

* Choose the closest meaning to the underlined.

1. As Le Gros Clark has put it, a stable[21] civilization will be built only on the foundations of the farm and the kitchen.
   a. laid　　b. described　　c. discussed　　d. set

2. The persons participated in the project were ill after eating the completely innocuous meal.
   a. harmless　　b. harmful　　c. beneficial　　d. tasteful

* Choose the best suitable word instead of the following underlined according to the context of the above article.

1. The machine it will not function without the right fuel in adequate qualities.
   a. quantities　　b. features　　c. characteristics　　d. traits

2. We consume food for what perhaps may be called its psychological affect.
   a. efficiency　　b. substance　　c. effect　　d. element

3. The majority of the 'guinea pigs' were so effected psychologically that they were ill after eating the completely innocuous meal.
   a. affected　　b. treated　　c. provoked　　d. diagnosed

---

21 stable: firmly established

* Fill in the blanks with a proper word, choosing it from given words. And answer the questions.

Certain chemical elements are necessary in small quantities—(   ) for bone, minute quantities of (   ) for teeth, small quantities of (   ) for healthy red blood. A (   ) diet, even if pronounced adequate, will not necessarily maintain the full vigour of either individual or <u>nation</u>, however satisfactory it may be during stress, as in wartime.

〈iodine, calcium, iron, carbohydrate, protein, diverse, monotonous〉

1. Put the above underlined into Korean.

2. flavour, vigour라는 어휘사용으로 미루어 보아 글쓴이는 어느 나라 영어를 사용하는지 고르시오.

   a. Australian English b. American English
   c. Canadian English d. British English

Pronunciation Tips

● **숫자 읽기**

자리수를 기준으로, 컴마 앞부터 끊어 각 컴마 단위로 읽는다.

1. 100,250,430: one hundred **million**, two hundred fifty **thousand**, four hundred thirty

2. 123,456,789: one hundred twenty three million, four hundred fifty six thousand, seven hundred eighty nine

3. 26.78 USD: twenty six dollars seventy eight cents (twenty six seventy eight)

4. 분수를 읽을 때 분자는 기수로, 분모는 서수로 읽으며 분자가 2이상일 경우 분모에 -s를 붙여 읽는다. 그러나 ½은 보통 a half, ¼은 a quarter로 읽는다. ⅔ two thirds, 2¾은 two and three quarters

   ex) By 1927, two-thirds of New York's twenty thousand lawyers were Jewish.[22]

22 Bryson 149쪽 참조.

Unit 12

12-1.

Prometheus and Pandora

Before earth and sea and heaven were created, all things wore one aspect, to which we give the name of Chaos — a confused and shapeless mass, nothing but[1] dead weight, in which, however, slumbered[2] the seeds of things. Earth, sea, and air were all mixed up together, so the earth was not solid,[3] the sea was not fluid,[4] and the air was not transparent.[5] God and Nature at last interposed[6] and put an end[7] to this discord,[8] separating earth from sea, and heaven from both. The fiery[9] part, being the lightest, sprang[10] up, and formed the skies; the air was next in weight and place.[11] The earth, being heavier, sank below; and

---

1 nothing but: only
2 slumbered (싹틀 줄 모르고) 잠들다 sleep
3 solid 고체의 hard, firm
4 fluid 액체의, 유동체의
5 transparent 투명한 (반) opaque
6 interposed 개입, 간섭하다 interfere, intervene. He interposed his authority. (그는 권한을 이용하여 간섭했다.)
7 pur an end: finish
8 discord 불화, 불일치 (반) accord, harmony
9 fiery 불타는
10 솟아올랐다 (v) spring-sprang-sprung
11 place 자리 잡다, 놓여 지다

the water took the lowest place, and buoyed[12] up the earth.

Here some god gave his good offices[13] in arranging and disposing[14] the earth. He appointed rivers and bays their places, raised mountains, scooped out valleys, distributed woods, fountains, fertile fields, and stony plains. The air being cleared, the stars began to appear, fishes took possession of the sea, birds of the air, and four-footed beasts of the land.

But a nobler animal was wanted, and Man was made. Prometheus took some of this earth, and kneading[15] it up with water, made man in the image[16] of gods. He gave him an upright stature, so that while all other animals turn their faces downward, and look to the earth, he raises his to heaven, and gazes on the stars.

Prometheus was one of the Titans, who inhabited the earth before the creation of man. To him and his brother Epimetheus was committed[17] the office of making man, and providing him and all other animals with the faculties necessary for their preservation, such gifts as wings to one, claws to another, a shelly covering to a third, etc. But when man came to be provided for, who was to be superior to all other animals, Epimetheus had been so prodigal[18] of his resources that he had nothing left to bestow upon him. In his perplexity he resorted to[19] his brother Prometheus, who, with the aid of Minerva (Athena), went up to heaven, and lighted his torch at the chariot of

12 buoy[bu:i] 뜨게 하다
13 offices 직책, 직분들
14 dispose 배치하다
15 knead 반죽하다, 개다, 주무르다
16 관련어 imagine, imagination
17 commit 위임하다, 맡기다
18 prodigal 낭비하는, 아낌없이 주는
19 resorted to 의지하다, 도움을 청하다

the sun, and brought down fire to man. With this gift man was more than a match for all other animals. It enabled him to make weapons wherewith subdue them; tools with which to cultivate[20] the earth; to warm his dwelling, so as to be comparatively independent of climate; and finally to introduce the arts and to coin money, the means of trade and commerce.

Woman was not yet made. The story is that Jupiter (Zeus) made her, and sent her to Prometheus and his brother, to punish them for their presumption in stealing fire from heaven; and man, for accepting the gift. The first woman was named Pandora. She was made in heaven, every god contributing something to perfect her. Venus (Aphrodite) gave her beauty, Mercury (Hermes) persuasion, Apollo music, etc. Thus equipped, she was conveyed to earth, and presented to Epimetheus, who gladly accepted her, though cautioned by his brother to beware of Jupiter and his gifts. Epimetheus had in his house a jar, in which were kept certain noxious[21] articles for which, in fitting man for his new abode, he had had no occasion.[22] Pandora was seized with an eager curiosity to know what this jar contained; and one day she slipped off the cover and looked in. Forthwith[23] there escaped a multitude of plagues[24] for hapless[25] man, — such as gout,[26] rheumatism, and colic[27] for his body, and envy, spite,[28] and revenge for his mind, — and scattered themselves far and wide. Pandora hastened to replace the lid! But the whole contents of the jar had escaped, one thing only excepted,

20 cultivate 경작하다. till이 동사로 쓰일 경우 비슷한 뜻이다. culture는 cultivate의 뜻에서 유래했다.
21 noxious: very harmful
22 had had no occasion (그 해로운 것들을 사용할) 경우가 없더라도. had had는 가정법 과거완료
23 forthwith 곧, 즉시
24 plagues 전염병, 재앙
25 hapless: unfortunate, unlucky
26 gout[gaut] 통풍, 응혈
27 colic 복통, 배앓이
28 spite 악의(malice), 심술, 원한(grudge), 앙심

which lay at the bottom, and that was *hope*. So, whatever evils are abroad, hope never entirely leaves us; and while we have *that*, no amount of other ills can makes us completely wretched.[29]

—Adapted from *Bulfinch's Mythology: The Age of Fable* (pp. 13–15)

29 wretched: miserable

Exercise

* Answer the questions.

1. Discuss "Chaos and Cosmos."

2. What is the opposite word of "fertile"?

3. Choose the word which is not have the meaning of "inhabit."
   a. live b. dwell c. reside d. accustom

4. Find the closest meaning with the word, "subdue."
   a. conquer b. escape c. overcome d. oppress

5. What did Prometheus bring down to man?
   a. water b. chariot c. fire d. tools

6. Why did Jupiter make and send a woman to Prometheus and his loving man?
   a. To punish them b. To make the happy
   c. To make him respect d. To make them mad

* Choose the closest meaning to the underlined.

1. Prometheus <u>inhabited</u> the earth before the creation of man.
   a. left b. lived c. cultivated d. destroyed

2. To Prometheus and his brother Epimetheus was committed the <u>office</u> of making man.
   a. working place b. method c. duty d. authority

3. Epimetheus had been so prodigal of his resources that he had nothing left to bestow upon him.

a. wear　　b. interpose　　c. promise　　d. give

4. In his perplexity he resorted to his brother Prometheus.

a. anxiety　　b. happiness　　c. sadness　　d. embarrassment

5. Independent of climate we can live on the earth.

a. Thanks to　　b. Regardless of　　c. Owing to　　d. Depending on

*** Translate the following sentences into Korean, referring to the example below.**

ex) serv(라틴어원): keep; reserve, conservation (cf. 부록(Appendix) 참조)

1. Can you think of anyone who is more deserving of happiness?

2. Man's chief purpose is the creation and preservation of values.

12-2.

The Cause of the Trojan War

The evil goddess of Discord,[1] Eris, was naturally not popular in Olympus, and when the gods gave a banquet they were apt to leave her out. Resenting this deeply, she determined to make trouble—and she succeeded very well indeed. At an important marriage, that of King Peleus and the sea nymph Thetis,[2] to which she alone of all the divinities[3] was not invited, she threw into the banqueting hall a golden apple marked *For the Fairest.* Of course all the goddesses wanted it, but in the end the choice was narrowed down to three: Aphrodite,[4] Hera[5] and Pallas Athena.[6] They asked Zeus to judge between them, but very wisely he refused to have anything to do with the matter. He told them to go to Mount Ida, near Troy, where the young prince Paris, also called Alexander, was keeping his father's sheep. He was an excellent judge of beauty, Zeus told them. Paris, though a royal prince, was doing shepherd's work

---

1 discord: disagreement; strife
2 Thetis[θetəs] (그리스 신화) 테티스(Peleus와의 사이에 Achilles를 낳음)
3 divinities: gods
4 Aphrodite[æfrədaiti] 아프로디테(사랑과 미의 여신; 로마신화의 Venus에 해당)
5 Hera[herə] 헤라(Zeus 신의 아내; 로마신화의 Juno)
6 Athena[əθi:nə] = Athene (그리스 신화) 아테네(지혜, 예술, 전술의 여신) cf. Minerva

because his father Priam, the King of Troy, had been warned that this prince would some day be the ruin of his country, and so had sent him away. At the moment Paris was living with a lovely nymph named Oenone.

His amazement can be imagined when there appeared before him the wondrous forms of the great goddesses. He was not asked, however, to gaze at the radiant[7] divinities and choose which of them seemed to him the fairest, but only to consider the bribes each offered and choose which seemed to him best worth taking. Nevertheless, the choice was not easy. What men care for most was set before him. Hera promised to make him Lord of Europe and Asia; Athena, that he would lead the Trojans to victory against the Greeks and lay Greece in ruins; Aphrodite, that the fairest woman in all the world should be his. Paris, a weakling and something of a coward, too, as later events showed, choose the last. He gave Aphrodite the golden apple.

That was the Judgment of Paris, famed everywhere as the real reason why the Trojan War was fought.

The fairest woman in the world was Helen, the daughter of Zeus and Leda. Such was the report of her beauty that not a young prince in Greece but wanted to marry her. When her suitors assembled in her home to make a formal proposal for her hand they were so many and from such powerful families that her reputed father, King Tyndareus, was afraid to select one among them, fearing that the others would unite against him. He therefore exacted first a solemn oath from all that they would champion the cause of Helen's husband, whoever he might be, if any wrong was done to him through his marriage. It was, after all, to each man's advantage to take the oath, since each was hoping he would be the person chosen, so they all bound themselves

7 radiant: bright

to punish to the uttermost anyone who carried or tried to carry Helen away. Then Tyndareus chose Menelaus, the brother of Agamemnon, and made him King of Sparta as well.

So matter stood when Paris gave the golden apple to Aphrodite. The Goddess of Love and Beauty knew very well where the most beautiful woman on earth was to be found. She led the young shepherd, with never a thought of Oenone left forlorn,[8] straight to Sparta, where Menelaus and Helen received him graciously as their guest. The ties between guest and host were strong. Each was bound to help and never harm the other. But Paris broke that sacred bond. Menelaus trusting completely to it left Paris in his home and went off to Crete. Then,

> Paris who coming
> Entered a friend's kind dwelling,
> Shamed the hand there that gave him food,
> Stealing away a woman.

Menelaus got back to find Helen gone, and he called upon all Greece to help him. The chieftains[9] responded, as they were bound to do. They came eager for the great enterprise, to cross the sea and lay mighty Troy in ashes. Two, however, of the first rank, were missing: Odysseus, King of the Island of Ithaca, and Achilles, the son of Peleus and the sea nymph Thetis. Odysseus, who was one of the shrewdest[10] and most sensible men in Greece, did not want to leave his house and family to embark on a romantic adventure overseas for

8 forlorn: abandoned; desperate; hopeless
9 chieftains 지휘관들
10 shrewd: sensible; discriminating

the sake of a faithless woman. He pretended, therefore, that he had gone mad, and when a messenger from the Greek Army arrived, the King was plowing a field and sowing it with salt instead of seed. But the messenger was shrewd too. He seized Odysseus' little son and put him directly in the way of the plough. Instantly the father turned the plough aside, thus proving that he had all his wits about him. However reluctant, he had to join the army.

Achilles was kept back by his mother. The sea nymph knew that if he went to Troy he was fated to die there. She sent him to the court of Lycomedes, the king who had treacherously killed Theseus, and made him wear women's clothes and hide among the maidens. Odysseus was dispatched[11] by the chieftains to find him out. Disguised as a pedlar[12] he went to court where the lad was said to be, with gay ornaments in his pack such as women love, and also some fine weapons. While the girls flocked around the trinkets,[13] Achilles fingered the swords and daggers. Odysseus knew him then, and he had no trouble at all in making him disregard what his mother said and go to the Greek camp with him.

—Adapted from *Mythology* (pp. 179-82)

11 dispatch: sent off to a destination or for a purpose

12 pedlar: travelling vendor of small wares

13 trinkets 장신구들

Exercise

* Choose the closest meaning to the underlined.

1. Resenting this deeply, she determined to make trouble.
   a. Angered by b. Feared by c. Pleased by d. Terrified by

2. They came eager for the great enterprise, to cross the sea and lay mighty Troy in ashes.
   a. launching b. plan c. embarkation d. fancy

* Answer the questions.

1. What is the Judgment of Paris? And discuss it.

2. Helen was fairest woman in the world. Explain the term, Hellenism, and think about the relation with the fairest one.

3. What did Odysseus think of Helen?

4. Explain Odysseus' pretense and Achilles' disguise.

12-3.

Humankind

Man's chief purpose is the creation and preservation of values: that is what gives meaning to our civilisation, and the participation in this is what gives significance, ultimately, to the individual human life.

Only in so far as values are fostered[1]—through art and religion and science and love and domestic life—can men effectively use the machines and powers that have enabled them to tame nature and secure human existence from the worst outrages[2] and accidents that forever threaten it. Civilization, our very capacity to be human, rests on that perpetual effort. If any nation or group thinks that the job is finished, or if man puts his confidence solely in the instruments and forgets the ends and ideals and metaphysical purposes—then the structure crumbles[3] away: then man himself is finished.

Thought, social relations, economic practices, biological activities, cosmic[4] backgrounds—all these are organically united and call for cooperations that

---

1 foster: promote growth of; encourage or harbour feeling
2 outrage: deed of violence
3 crumble: press or crush into fragments
4 cosmic: of the universe

reach out beyond the borders of any single community, even as they reach out beyond our limited present, into the past and future. That which exists by itself has, indeed, no real existence at all; it is a phantasm,[5] an aberration[6] of the mind. The finer life becomes, the more complicated becomes the network of relationships, and the more invisible filaments[7] bind part with part.

Goethe[8] once put this truth admirably in a conversation with Eckermann.[9] "People," he said, "are always talking about originality; but what do they mean? As soon as we are born, the world begins to work upon us, and keeps on to the end. What can we call ours except energy, strength, will? If I could give an account of what I owe to great predecessors and contemporaries,[10] there would be but a small remainder." That does not merely hold for Goethe; it holds for every human group, every community, every person.

The individual who fancies he has made his own professional career, or the inventor who believes he has the sole right to his invention, or the business man who thinks his own unaided efforts have brought him his fortune is merely ignorant of his debts. Like Bounderby, who Dickens[11] portrayed in *Hard Times*, he is a monster of ingratitude. Darwin[12] formulated his *Origin of Species* with

---

5 phantasm: illusion

6 aberration: derivation from type; intellectual deficiency

7 filament: fibre; slender thread-like body

8 Johann Wolfgang von Goethe (1749-1832) was a German writer and statesman.

9 Johann Peter Eckermann (1792-1854), German poet and author, is best known for his work *Conversations with Goethe*, the fruit of his association with Johann Wolfgang von Goethe during the last years of Goethe's life.

10 predecessors and contemporaries 선행자들(앞서 살았던 사람들)과 동시대인들(함께 살고 있는 사람들)

11 Charles John Huffam Dickens (1812-1870) was an English writer and social critic. He created some of the world's most well-known fictional characters and is generally regarded as the greatest novelist of the Victorian period. During his life, his works enjoyed unprecedented popularity, and by the twentieth century he was widely seen as a literary genius by critics and scholars. His novels and short stories continue to be widely popular.

12 Charles Robert Darwin (1809-1882) was an English naturalist and geologist, best known for his

the sense that he was making a completely unique discovery. Before he was finished the similar hypothesis[13] of another young naturalist, Wallace,[14] was brought to his attention: it turned out that they had both got their clue from Malthus's *Essay on Population.*[15] By the time Darwin published his second edition, he had at last become aware of a whole line of predecessors and partial anticipators,[16] extending back to the Greeks.

—Lewis Mumford: *Faith for Living from A University Anthology for Overseas Students* (pp. 293-95)

---

contributions to evolutionary theory. He established that all species of life have descended over time from common ancestors, and in a joint publication with Alfred Russel Wallace introduced his scientific theory that this branching pattern of evolution resulted from a process that he called natural selection, in which the struggle for existence has a similar effect to the artificial selection involved in selective breeding.

13 hypothesis: supposition made as basis for reasoning 가설

14 Alfred Russel Wallace (1823-1913) was a British naturalist, explorer, geographer, anthropologist, and biologist. He is best known for independently conceiving the theory of evolution through natural selection; his paper on the subject was jointly published with some of Charles Darwin's writings in 1858. This prompted Darwin to publish his own ideas in *On the Origin of Species.* Wallace did extensive fieldwork, first in the Amazon River basin and then in the Malay Archipelago, where he identified the faunal divide now termed the Wallace Line, which separates the Indonesian archipelago into two distinct parts: a western portion in which the animals are largely of Asian origin, and an eastern portion where the fauna reflect Australasia.

15 The Reverend Thomas Robert Malthus (1766-1834) was an English cleric and scholar, influential in the fields of political economy and demography. His *An Essay on the Principle of Population* observed that sooner or later population will be checked by famine and disease, leading to what is known as a Malthusian catastrophe. He wrote in opposition to the popular view in 18th century Europe that saw society as improving and in principle as perfectible. He thought that the dangers of population growth precluded progress towards a utopian society: "The power of population is indefinitely greater than the power in the earth to produce subsistence for man." As a cleric, Malthus saw this situation as divinely imposed to teach virtuous behaviour.

16 at last become aware of a whole line of predecessors and partial anticipators 결국 모든 선임자들과 약간의 예상가들을 인식하게 되었다

Grammatical Tips

● **분사(Participle)**

분사는 목적어를 갖는 타동사에 -ing나 -ed(규칙변화 동사)를 붙이는 형태다.

1. 현재분사: 타동사+ing(주는) tiring, boring, exciting, amusing

2. 과거분사: 타동사+ed(받는) tired, interested, bored, excited, amused

Cafes are *boring*. (= Cafes bore me. I feel *bored* in them.)
My date last night was *boring*. (= My date bored me. He wasn't interesting.)

I get *bored* in cafes.
(= Cafes bore me. I have a feeling of boredom when I go to them.)

The *interesting* show made the audience *amused*.
(interesting show 재미를 주는 쇼, amused 관객들이 재미를 받는)

I was not *interested* in Professor Kim's *boring* lecture.

3. 강조의 현재분사(-ing가 very의 뜻으로 쓰인다)

It is freezing cold (perishing cold, burning hot, scorching hot).
I'm exceeding glad.

4. 부사절을 분사구문으로 전환할 때 접속사와 종속절의 주어가 주절의 주어와 같을 때 보통 생략한다.

While I was walking along the street, I met a friend of mine.
= Walking along the street, I met a friend of mine.

If you turn to the right, you will find the vending machine.
= Turning to the right, you will find the vending machine.

5. 현재분사는 능동이고 과거분사는 수동이다.

Though they knew the danger, they pushed on.
= Knowing the danger, they pushed on.

When she was left to herself, she began to cry.
= Left to herself, she began to cry.

6. 종속절이 주절과 같은 시제이면 단순분사, 주절보다 앞선 시제이면 완료분사로 나타낸다.

When I visited him yesterday, he lent this book to me.
= I visiting him yesterday, he lent this book to me.

As I had lost my wallet, I could not buy the book.
= Having lost my wallet, I could not buy the book.

Exercise

* 다음 질문에 답하시오.

1. 윗글에서 필자의 의도를 잘 나타내고 있는 다음 문장을 우리말로 옮기시오.

   If man puts his confidence solely in the instruments and forgets the ends and ideals and metaphysical purposes—then the structure crumbles away: then man himself is finished.

2. 필자가 독일 문학자인 괴테와 영국의 생물학자인 다윈을 언급하는 이유를 설명하시오.

* Read the following passage and answer the questions.

"As societies become technologically sophisticated, rates of abortion often rise, thereby lowering the life expectancy rate of the population (assuming that life expectancy is calculated from the point of conception rather than at birth). In some parts of the world, often in those parts of the world where reproductive success and large families are valued, early childhood is a relatively dangerous time of life. In other places, often in high-tech places where small families are valued and the womb is no longer thought of as a sanctified ground, the real dangers come earlier in life, and if you are an unwanted child, the womb can be hazardous to your health."

—From "Moral Maps, "First World" Conceits, and the New Evangelists,"
Richard A. Shweder, *Culture Matters* (p. 166)

*** 위 글과 관련하여 다음 진술이 맞는지 그른지 밝히시오.**

1. 산업사회로 발전할수록 유산율이 높다. (　　)
2. 사람들의 기대 수명도 낮아진다. (　)
3. 기대수명은 임신시점이 아니라 출산시점으로 가정한다. (　)
4. 소규모 가족에 가치를 두는 첨단사회에서 여성의 자궁은 신성하게 여겨지지 않는다. (　)
5. 임신과 출산을 하지 않는 여성의 자궁은 그 여성의 건강에 해를 끼칠 수 있다. (　)

Unit 13

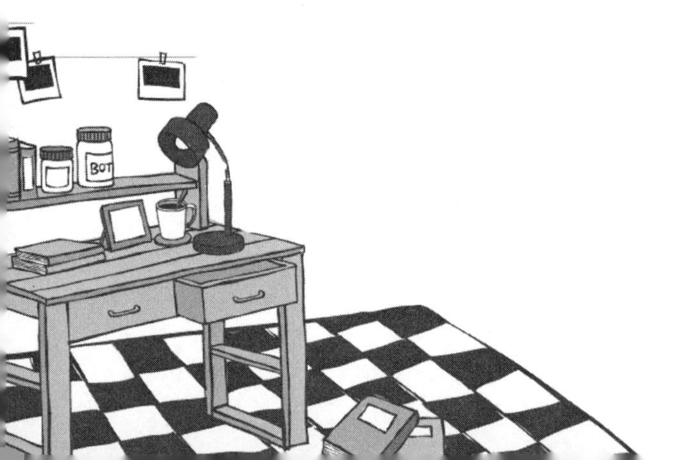

13-1.

He Loved Me Truly

—Bernadine Bailey & Dorothy Walworth

The bride rode with her husband on the high front seat on the jolting[1] wagon. She was thirty one years old. In 1819 that was middle-aged, for most pioneer women died early. It was a cold December day, and they were headed north toward forest country.

Yesterday Tom had come to her house in Elizabethtown, Kentucky, all the way from his Indiana farm. He had come straight to the point: "Miss Sally, I have no wife and you no husband. I came a purpose[2] to marry you. I knowed[3] you from a girl and you knowed me from a boy. I've no time to lose. If you're willing, let it be done straight off."[4]

That morning they had been married. The preacher[5] wrote down that she, Sarah Bush Johnston, had been three years a widow, and that Tom's wife had died last winter. The horses and wagon Tom had borrowed waited outside. The

1 jolting 덜컹거리는
2 a purpose: with a purpose
3 knowed: knew의 오용. 말하는 사람, 즉 Tom이 교육받지 못했음을 나타낸다.
4 straight off 바로, 당장에
5 preacher: priest, reverend

wagon was piled high with her household goods, so that there was scarcely room for her three children. Tom had two children of his own. He hadn't told them he was bringing back a new mother. There was a shadow in Sarah's steady blue eyes when she thought about that. Maybe they'd feel she didn't really belong.[6]

A raft[7] ferried[8] the wagon across the half-frozen Ohio River. The air became colder; the wheels sank[9] in the snow. After five days they came to a log cabin in a small clearing.[10] It had no windows, and the door was only a deerskin-covered opening.

Tom called and a little boy ran out of the door. He was thin as a scarecrow[11] and wore ragged shirt and tattered deerskin pants. The look in his eyes went to Sarah's heart. She got down from the wagon, opened her arms and folded him close.

"I reckon[12] we'll be good friends," she said. "Howdy, Abe Lincoln." She had never been in the wilderness before; she had known small town comfort. This was a one-room cabin. Its floors were hard packed dirt. The bedstead[13] was crudely made of boards, with a mattress of loose cornhusk.[14] The bedcovers were skins and castoff[15] clothing. Ten-year-old Abe and his twelve-year-old sister slept on piles of leaves up in the loft.[16] They climbed up

6 belong 어울리다
7 raft 뗏목
8 ferry 수송하다
9 sink-sank-sunk
10 clearing 개간지, 개활지
11 scarecrow 허수아비
12 reckon: think
13 bedstead 침대 틀
14 cornhusk 옥수수 껍질
15 castoff 버려진
16 loft (건초) 다락, 더그매

to it by means of pegs[17] fastened to the wall.

The furniture was a few three-legged stools and a table axed smooth on top. Dennis Hanks, an 18-year-old cousin of Tom's first wife, Nancy Hanks, was living with the family. He had been trying to cook with a Dutch oven, one battered[18] pot and a couple of[19] iron spoons.

Although she must have expected a place far better than this, all Sarah said was, "Tom, fetch me a load of firewood. I have to heat some water."

This new stepmother with the rosy face and the bright curly hair wasted no time. As soon as the water steamed, she brought out of her own belongings a gourd[20] full of homemade soap. Then, in front of hot fire, she scrubbed[21] Abe and his sister and combed their matted[22] hair with her own shell comb.[23]

When the wagon was unpacked, little Abe, who had not said a word, ran his bony fingers over such wonderful things as a walnut bureau,[24] a clothes chest,[25] a loom[26] and reel[27] chairs. That night when he went to bed in the loft he did not find the leaves. Sarah had thrown them outdoors. In their place was a feather mattress, a feather pillow and warm blankets.

In a couple of weeks, a boy wouldn't have known the place. Sarah worked hard, and she could make other people work, too—even Tom. He

---

17 pegs 나무 못
18 battered 찌그러진
19 a couple of: two
20 gourd[guərd, gɔ:rd]: bowl
21 scrub 문질러 닦다
22 matted 헝클어진
23 b는 묵음(silent sound). ex. dumb, climb
24 walnut bureau 호두나무 옷장
25 chest 장롱
26 loom 베틀
27 reel 얼레

meant well but was likely to[28] let things slide. She never said he must do thus and so. She was too wise and gentle. But somehow Tom found himself making a real door and window for the cabin. He laid a floor, filled the cracks[29] between logs, white washed[30] the inside walls.

Sarah wove[31] homespun[32] cloth and made for shirts for Abe, coloring them with dye[33] she steeped[34] out of roots and herbs. She made him deerskin breeches[35] that fitted, moccasins[36] and a coonskin[37] cap. She held her mirror so he could see himself for the first time—and he said, "Land o' Goshen,[38] is that me?"

Sometimes in the early mornings when Sarah laid a new fire in the ashes, she got to thinking it was queer[39] how things had come about.[40] When Tom Lincoln had courted[41] her 14 years ago, she had turned him down[42] for Daniel Johnston. Tom had been married to Nancy Hanks, who had died. Now, after all these years, Tom and she were together again, with his children and her children to feed and care for.

---

28 be likely to: be apt to
29 cracks 갈라진 틈
30 white washed 깨끗하게 다듬다
31 weave-wove-woven (직물, 천을) 짜다
32 homespun 수직물의, 손으로 짠
33 dye 염료
34 steeped 적시다
35 breeches: pants
36 moccasins 가죽 신
37 coonskin 너구리 가죽
38 Land o' Goshen (성경) 낙토, 야아!
39 queer: strange, peculiar
40 come about: bring about, happen
41 court: propose
42 turn down: refuse, reject

The cabin was 18 feet square and there were eight people under its shabby[43] roof. Somehow, Sarah felt, she must make them into a family that loved each other and felt as if they had always been together. There was plenty of[44] chance for trouble, with two sets of young ones who had never laid eyes on[45] each other till now. Those first weeks, Sarah felt mighty[46] anxious, especially about Abe.

Maybe, if it hadn't been for her, Abe wouldn't have lived to be a man. He had always grown so fast and never had enough to eat. But now, when he had eaten enough johnnycake[47] and meat and potatoes that were cooked through, not just burned on top, he stopped looking so pinched.[48] He wasn't so quiet anymore. Now that he had some flesh[49] on his bones, he was fuller of fun than anybody. He learned to tell yarns,[50] like his father.

Sometimes Sarah thought that she loved Abe more than her own children. But it was just that she knew, deep down in her heart, that Abe was somebody special who didn't belong to her but was hers to keep for a while.

When Abe was little, Tom hadn't minded his going to school. But now that the boy was older and stronger, Tom didn't see why he shouldn't stay home and chop down trees and thresh[51] wheat or hire out[52] to the neighbors for husking corn[53] at 30 cents a day. Of course, he felt proud when the

---

43 shabby: poor
44 plenty of: lots of, a lot of
45 lay eyes on ~에 눈이 가다, 주목vi
46 mighty: pretty
47 johnnycake: corn bread
48 pinched 오그라들다
49 flesh (신체의) 살, 살집
50 tell yarns: tell stories
51 thresh 타작하다
52 hire out 노동자로 고용되다
53 husking corn 옥수수 껍질 벗기기

neighbors came to have Abe write their letters. The boy used the pen he had made from a buzzard's quill[54] and the ink he'd made from brierroot.[55] But Abe was "reaching too far" when he spent so much time reading books. Tom told Abe a man didn't need to know so almighty much to get along.[56]

If Sarah hadn't taken Abe's part against his father, Abe wouldn't have had as much schooling as he did, though goodness knows it wasn't much.[57] Abe would rather read than eat. He'd read in the morning, as soon as it was light enough to see. He'd read in the evening when the chores[58] were done. He walked 17 miles to borrow books from Lawyer Pitcher at Rockport: *Aesop's Fables*, *Robinson Crusoe*, *Pilgrim's Progress*, *Shakespeare*, *The Statutes of Indiana*.[59]

When a book he'd borrowed was rained on, he worked three full days to pay for it. Once he gave man 50 cents for an old barrel[60] and found at the bottom of it Blackstone's *Commentaries*,[61] a famous book on law. You'd think he'd found a gold mine. He began reading late at night by the fire. When Tom complained, Sarah said, "Leave the boy be." She always let him read as long as he wanted to. If he fell asleep there on the floor, she would get a quilt[62] and wrap it gently around him.

---

54 buzzard's quill 매의 깃
55 brier 야생장미
56 get along 살아가다
57 though goodness knows it wasn't much 학교 교육을 많이 받은 것이 아님에도
58 chores 잡일, routine works
59 fable 우화, pilgrim 성지순례자, statute 법령
60 barrel 통
61 *Commentaries* 주석서
62 quilt 누비이불

He did his arithmetic[63] with charcoal on board. When the board got to black, he'd scrape it off and start again. If he read something he liked a lot, he'd write it down. He was always writing and was always running out of paper. After he wrote something, he'd read it loud to Sarah by the fire, after Tom and the rest had gone to bed. "Did I make it plain? he always asked her. She answered him as well as anybody who didn't know how to read or write.

They told each other things they told nobody else. He had dark spells[64] when he thought it was no use to hope and to plan. But Sarah knew Abe needed a lot of encouraging.

In 1830 Tom decided to look for better farmland in Illinois. Abe helped his father build the two-room cabin where Sarah and Tom were to spend the rest of their lives. The place was hardly built when the time came for Abe to leave home. He was now a grown man, 22 years old. He had a chance to clerk in Denton Offut's store over in New Salem.

At first he came home often. After he became a lawyer, he visited there twice a year. Every time Sarah saw him, it seemed as if his mind was bigger. Other folks' mind got to a place and then stopped, but Abe's kept on growing. He told her about his law cases, about his going to the state legislature[65] and his marrying Mary Todd. After Tom died, 1851, Abe saw to it that[66] Sarah didn't want[67] for anything.

When she heard Abe was going to Charleston for his fourth debate with Stephen A. Douglas, she went there, without saying a word to Abe. It would be

---

63 arithmetic 산수. cf. algebra 대수

64 dark spells 어두운 시절

65 the state legislature (일리노이)주 의회

66 see to it that ~하도록 조처하다

67 want 부족하다

enough—it had always been enough—just to watch him. She was one of the crowd on the street as the parade went by. There was a big float[68] drawn by oxen, carrying three men splitting rails and a sign, "Honest Abe, the Rail Splitter."[69]

Now here he came, riding in a shiny black carriage, and tipping[70] his tall black hat right and left. Was that her Abe? She tried to make herself small, but he saw her, made the carriage stop. Then, right in front everybody, he got out of the carriage, came over, put his arms around her and kissed her. Yes, that was her Abe.

She wasn't the crying kind, but alone where nobody could see her, she cried when he was elected President. In the winter of 1861, before he went to Washington, he crossed the state to see her and to say goodbye, coming by train and carriage in the mud and slush.[71] He brought her some fine black cloth for a dress. It was really too beautiful to put scissors into. She'd take it out and feel it once in a while.[72]

Abe looked tired. He had a lot on his mind, but they had a fine talk. Even when they were silent, they still said things to each other, and he still had respect for what she thought. When he kissed her goodbye, he said he'd see her soon. But somehow she knew she wouldn't see him again.

Four years later, they came and told her he was dead. The newspapers wrote the longest piece about his real mother. That was as it should be. But some folks came and asked her what sort of boy Abe had been. She wanted to

---

68 float 장식 수레
69 the Rail Splitter 울타리의 가로대를 만드는 사람, 링컨의 별명
70 tipping (인사로) 가볍게 손대면서
71 mud and slush 진흙탕
72 once in a while: sometimes, on and off, at times

tell them, but it was hard to find the words. "Abe was a good boy," she said. "He never gave me a cross[73] word or look." Then she added, "He loved me truly, I think."

Often, during the four years that remained to her, she would sit of an evening and think of Abe. She remembered him as a little boy. She was baking johnnycake for him. She was weaving him a shirt. She was covering him with a blanket when he had fallen asleep over his books.

Her death, on December 10, 1869, passed unnoticed by the nation. For many years she was not even mentioned by historians and biographers more recently, the graves of Thomas and Sarah were marked with a suitable stone. Their home site has been made into a state park, with a reproduction of the two-room cabin that Abe helped to build. Only in the last few years have Americans come to know that when Abraham Lincoln said, "All that I am owe to my angel mother," he was speaking of Sarah—his beloved stepmother.

—Adapted

* Abraham Lincoln (1809–1865) was the 16th president of the United States, serving from March 1861 until his assassination in April 1865. Lincoln led the United States through its Civil War—its bloodiest war and its greatest moral, constitutional and political crisis. In doing so, he preserved the Union, abolished slavery, strengthened the federal government, and modernized the economy.

In 1860 Lincoln secured the Republican Party presidential nomination as a moderate from a swing state. With very little support in the slave states, Lincoln swept the North and was elected president in 1860. His election prompted seven southern slave states

73 cross 가로지르는, 엇갈린, 짓궂은

to form the Confederacy before he took the office. No compromise or reconciliation was found regarding slavery.

His Gettysburg Address of 1863 became an iconic statement of America's dedication to the principles of nationalism, republicanism, equal rights, liberty, and democracy. Lincoln held a moderate view of Reconstruction, seeking to reunite the nation speedily through a policy of generous reconciliation in the face of lingering and bitter divisiveness. Six days after the surrender of Confederate commanding general Robert E. Lee, Lincoln was assassinated by John Wilkes Booth, a Confederate sympathizer.

Lincoln has been consistently ranked both by scholars and the public as one of the three greatest U.S. presidents.

13-2.

I Have a Dream

—Martin Luther King[1]

Martin Luther King's "I Have a Dream" speech on 28 August, 1963

I am happy to join with you today in what will go down in history as the greatest demonstration for freedom in the history of our nation.

Five score years ago, a great American, in whose symbolic shadow we stand today, signed the Emancipation Proclamation.[2] This momentous decree[3] came as a great beacon[4] light of hope to millions of Negro slaves[5] who had been seared[6] in the flames of withering[7] injustice. It came as a joyous daybreak

---

1 Martin Luther King, Jr. (1929–1968) was an American pastor, activist, humanitarian, and leader in the African-American Civil Rights Movement. He is best known for his role in the advancement of civil rights using nonviolent civil disobedience based on his Christian beliefs.

2 the Emancipation Proclamation 노예해방선언

3 momentous decree 중대한 포고

4 beacon 횃불

5 According to Bryson, "As early as 1775, [blacks] accounted for 40 percent of the population of Virginia, 30 percent in North Carolina, Maryland, and Georgia, and well over 60 percent in South Carolina." (Maldwyn Allen Jones, *American Immigration*, Chicago: U of Chicago P, 1960, pp. 32–35)

6 seared 그을린

7 withering 시들은, 위축된

to end the long night of captivity.[8]

But one hundred years later, the Negro still is not free. One hundred years later, the life of the Negro is still sadly crippled[9] by the manacles[10] of segregation[11] and the chains of discrimination. One hundred years later, the Negro lives on a lonely island of poverty in the midst of a vast ocean of material prosperity. One hundred years later, the Negro is still languished[12] in the corners of American society and finds himself in an exile in his own land. And so we have come here today to dramatize[13] a shameful condition.

In a sense we've come to our nation's Capital to cash a check.[14] When the architects of our republic wrote the magnificent words of the Constitution and the Declaration of Independence, they were signing a promissory note[15] to which every American was to fall heir. This note was a promise that all men, yes, black men as well as white men, would be guaranteed the unalienable rights of life, liberty, and the pursuit of happiness.[16]

It is obvious today that America has defaulted[17] on this promissory note insofar as her citizens of color are concerned. Instead of honoring this sacred obligation, America has given the Negro people a bad check; a check which has come back marked "insufficient funds."[18]

---

8 captivity 포박
9 crippled 절름거리다
10 manacles 족쇄
11 segregation 인종분리
12 languished 괴롭게 살다
13 dramatize 극적으로 표현하다
14 cash a check 어음을 현금으로 바꾸다
15 promissory note 약속어음
16 guaranteed the unalienable rights of life, liberty, and the pursuit of happiness 양도할 수 없는 권리인 삶, 자유, 행복추구권을 보증하는
17 defaulted 채무를 이행하지 않다, 부도를 내다
18 a check which has come back marked "insufficient funds" "잔고부족"이라고 표시되어 반송된 부도

But we refuse to believe that the bank of justice is bankrupt.[19] We refuse to believe that there are insufficient funds in the great vaults[20] of opportunity of this nation. And so, we have come to cash this check—a check that will give us upon demand the riches of freedom and the security of justice.

We have also come to this hallowed[21] spot to remind America of the fierce urgency[22] of Now. This is no time to engage in the luxury of cooling off or to take the tranquilizing drug of gradualism.[23] Now is the time to make real the promises of democracy. Now is the time to rise from the dark and desolate[24] valley of segregation to the sunlit path of racial justice. Now is the time to lift our nation from the quicksands[25] of racial injustice to the solid rock of brotherhood. Now is the time to make justice a reality for all of God's children.

It would be fatal for the nation to overlook the urgency of the moment. This sweltering[26] summer of the Negro's legitimate discontent will not pass until there is an invigorating[27] autumn of freedom and equality. Nineteen sixty-three is not an end, but a beginning. And those who hope that the Negro needed to blow off steam and will now be content will have a rude awakening[28] if the nation returns to business as usual. And there will be neither rest nor tranquility in America until the Negro is granted his citizenship rights. The whirlwinds of

---

수표

19 bankrupt 파산한 (n) bankruptcy

20 vaults 둥근 천장

21 hallowed 신성한 holy, sacred

22 fierce urgency 흉포한(모진, 격심한) 긴급, 절박

23 to take the tranquilizing drug of gradualism 점진주의라는 진정제를 복용하거나

24 desolate 황량한

25 quicksands 수렁

26 sweltering 찌는 듯이 더운

27 invigorating 상쾌한

28 a rude awakening 잠이 덜 깬, 비몽사몽의 상태

revolt will continue to shake the foundations of our nation until the bright day of justice emerges.

But there is something that I must say to my people who stand on the warm threshold which leads into the palace of justice. In the process of gaining our rightful place we must not be guilty of wrongful deeds. Let us not seek to satisfy our thirst for freedom by drinking from the cup of bitterness and hatred. We must forever conduct our struggle on the high plane of dignity and discipline. We must not allow our creative protest to degenerate[29] into physical violence. Again and again we must rise to the majestic heights of meeting physical force with soul force.

The marvelous new militancy[30] which has engulfed[31] the Negro community must not lead us to a distrust of all white people, for many of our white brothers, as evidenced by their presence here today, have come to realize that their destiny is tied up with our destiny. And they have come to realize that their freedom is inextricably[32] bound to our freedom. We cannot walk alone.

And as we walk, we must make the pledge[33] that we shall march ahead. We cannot turn back. There are those who are asking the devotees of civil rights, "When will you be satisfied?"

We can never be satisfied as long as the Negro is the victim of the unspeakable horrors of police brutality.

We can never be satisfied as long as our bodies, heavy with the fatigue of

---

29 degenerate 타락시키다

30 militancy 투쟁정신, 교전상태

31 engulfed 삼켜버리다, 가라앉히다

32 inextricably 떼려야 뗄 수 없이, 불가분의

33 pledge 서약, 보증

travel, cannot gain lodging in the motels of the highways and the hotels of the cities.

We cannot be satisfied as long as the Negro's basic mobility is from a smaller ghetto to a larger one.

We can never be satisfied as long as our children are stripped[34] of their selfhood and robbed of their dignity by signs stating: "For Whites Only."

We cannot be satisfied as long as a Negro in Mississippi cannot vote and a Negro in New York believes he has nothing for which to vote.

No, no, we are not satisfied, and we will not be satisfied until "justice rolls down like waters, and righteousness like a mighty stream."[35]

I am not unmindful that some of you have come here out of great trials and tribulations.[36] Some of you have come fresh from narrow jail cells. And some of you have come from areas where your quest for freedom left you battered by the storms of persecution and staggered by the winds of police brutality. You have been the veterans of creative suffering. Continue to work with the faith that unearned suffering is redemptive.

Go back to Mississippi, go back to Alabama, go back to South Carolina, go back to Georgia, go back to Louisiana, go back to the slums and ghettos of our northern cities, knowing that somehow this situation can and will be changed. Let us not wallow[37] in the valley of despair.

I say to you today, my friends. And so even though we face the difficulties of today and tomorrow, I still have a dream. It is a dream deeply rooted in the American dream.

---

34 stripped 제거하다, 벗겨내다

35 "justice ~ stream" 정의가 물처럼 그리고 공의가 도도한 강처럼 흐를 때까지 Amos 5:24

36 trials and tribulations 시련과 간난

37 wallow 뒹굴다, 빠지다

I have a dream that one day this nation will rise up and live out the true meaning of its creed: "We hold these truths to be self-evident; that all men are created equal."

I have a dream that one day on the red hills of Georgia, the sons of former slaves and the sons of former slave owners will be able to sit down together at the table of brotherhood.

I have a dream that one day even the state of Mississippi, a state sweltering with the heat of injustice, sweltering with the heat of oppression, will be transformed into an oasis of freedom and justice.

I have a dream that my four little children will one day live in a nation where they will not be judged by the color of their skin but by the content of their character.

I have a dream today.

I have a dream that one day, down in Alabama, with its vicious racists, with its governor having his lips dripping with the words of interposition[38] and nullification,[39] that one day right there in Alabama little black boys and black girls will be able to join hands with little white boys and white girls as sisters and brothers.

I have a dream today.

I have a dream that one day every valley shall be exalted,[40] every hill and mountain shall be made low, the rough places will be made plain, and the crooked places will be made straight, "and the glory of the Lord shall be revealed and all flesh shall see it together."[41]

---

38 interposition (미국의) 주권(州權) 우위설(주는 그 권한을 침해하는 연방정부의 조처에 반대할 수 있다는 설)

39 nullification 주의 연방법 효력[실시]의 거부

40 exalted 높이다

41 "and the glory ~ together" Isaiah 40:4-5

This is our hope. This is the faith that I go back to the South with. With this faith, we will be able to hew[42] out of the mountain of despair a stone of hope. With this faith, we will be able to transform the jangling discords of our nation into a beautiful symphony of brotherhood.

With this faith, we will be able to work together, to pray together, to struggle together, to go to jail together, to stand up for freedom together, knowing that we will be free one day.

And this will be the day when all of God's children will be able to sing with new meaning, "My country 'tis of thee, sweet land of liberty, of thee I sing. Land where my fathers died, land of the Pilgrims' pride, from every mountainside, let freedom ring."

And if America is to be a great nation, this must become true. And so let freedom ring from the prodigious[43] hilltops of New Hampshire. Let freedom ring from the mighty mountains of New York. Let freedom ring from the heightening Alleghenies[44] of Pennsylvania.

Let freedom ring from the snow-capped Rockies of Colorado. Let freedom ring from the curvaceous slopes of California. But not only that; let freedom ring from the Stone Mountain of Georgia. Let freedom ring from Lookout Mountain of Tennessee.

Let freedom ring from every hill and molehill of Mississippi. From every mountainside, let freedom ring.

And when this happens, and when we allow freedom ring, when we let it ring from every village and every hamlet, from every state and every city, we

42 hew 만들다, 깎아내다

43 prodigious 거대한, great

44 Alleghenies 앨러게이니 산맥(미국 동부의 Appalachian 산계의 일부)

will be able to speed up that day when all of God's children, black men and white men, Jews and gentiles, Protestants and Catholics, will be able to join hands and sing in the words of the old Negro spiritual, "Free at last! Free at last! Thank God Almighty, we are free at last!"

Exercise

* Fill in the blanks with a suitable word or phrase.

1. Abe felt proud when the neighbors came to have Abe ______ their letters.
   a. to write b. write c. written d. wrote

2. Abe helped his father ______ the two-room cabin where sarah and Tom were to spend the rest of their lives.
   a. built b. build c. to build d. building

3. Abe made the carriage ________.
   a. stop b. stopping c. to stop d. stopped

* 본문에서 가정법 문장들을 찾아 설명하고 가정법 과거, 과거완료와 직설법의 관계를 설명하시오.

* 아래 문장에서 주어와 동사를 찾고 의문문이 아닌 평서문에서 주어와 동사의 위치가 도치된 이유를 말하시오.

Only in the last few years have Americans come to know that when Abraham Lincoln said, "All that I am owe to my angel mother," he was speaking of Sarah—his beloved stepmother.

* Read the following passage and answer the questions.

The Constitution is more notable for what it does not include. Nowhere does it mention *slaves* or *slavery*. Slaves are referred to only as "all other persons," by which was meant those who were neither free nor Indian. For purposes of determining representation and taxation, each slave was counted as three-fifths of a person, an absurdity that was not lost on many of the delegates. "Upon what principle is it that slaves shall be computed in the representation?" Gouverneur Morris of Pennsylvania asked sarcastically during the debates. "Are they Men? Then make them Citizens and let them vote. Why then is there no other property included? The Houses in this City are worth more than all the wretched slaves which cover the rice swamps of South Carolina." The arrangement, he noted angrily, meant that "the inhabitant of Georgia and South Carolina who goes to the Coast of Africa, and in defiance of the most sacred laws of humanity tears away his fellow creatures from their dearest connections and damns them to the most cruel bondages shall have more votes in a Government instituted for protection of the rights of mankind than the citizen of Pennsylvania or New Jersey who views with a laudable horror so nefarious[45] a practice." Nonetheless, the compromise carried, as did a proposal by Roger Sherman of Connecticut to remove the words *slave* and *slavery* wherever they appeared.

The words *nation* and *national* also appear nowhere in the document, and again not by accident or oversight. Fearing that national smacked of[46] a system in which power was dangerously centralized, the delegates instead used the more neutral and less emotive *federal*, derived from the Latin *fides*, "faith," and in the eighteenth century still carrying the sense of a relationship resting on trust.

—Bryson, *Made in America* (pp. 56–57)

1. 의원선출과 징세를 위해 흑인 노예 한 명은 미국의 남북전쟁(the Civil War) 무렵까지 백인 한 사람 분으로 온전히 인정받지 못했던 사실을 기술한 부분을 찾아 쓰시오.

2. "흑인 노예들은 사람입니까? 그렇다면 그들을 시민으로 인정하고 그들이 투표하게 하십시오."라는 펜실베니아 모리스 주지사의 말을 찾아 쓰시오.

3. 미국 헌법에서 national이란 단어 대신에 federal이란 단어가 쓰인 이유를 찾아 쓰시오.

---

45 nefarious 못된, 사악한

46 smack of (vi) 맛이 나다: This meat smacks of garlic. 낌새가 있다, ~한 데가 있다: He smacks of the stage. 그는 무대 배우 같은 데가 있다.

Unit 14

14-1. *An Interview*

14-2. *The Great Stone Face*

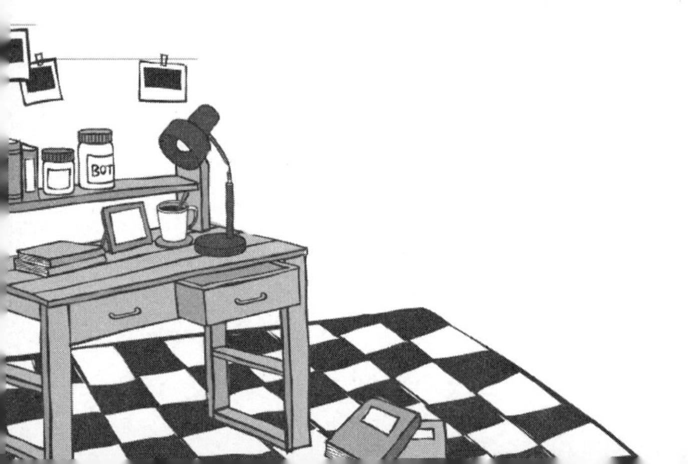

14-1.

An Interview

In applying for a job, one should always keep in mind the old truth— "First impressions are lasting." Your prospective employer[1] is going to judge you by your appearance, your bearing, and above all, by your speech. Before hiring someone for a position, an employer naturally wants to have an interview. The interview gives him a chance to size up the applicant. Most large companies have trained specialists, called personnel managers, whose job it is to interview and pass judgment on prospective employees. The personnel specialist can usually make fairly accurate judgments about an applicant's character through means of the interview.

The interview begins the moment one raps[2] on the personnel manager's office door. The person who barges into[3] the interviewer's office without bothering to knock has already made a bad impression. The rules of common courtesy are never more important than when presenting oneself for an

1 prospective employer 장래 고용주
2 rap: knock
3 barge into~ 난폭하게 ~에 들어가다

interview. The skillful interviewer, however, will try to put the applicant at ease. He has a sincere desire to discover whether the applicant has qualities that will make him an asset to the company. In spite of the fact that many jobs require specific skills and talents, however, probably the most valuable asset that one can display when applying for a job is a well-developed personality.

During an interview one should be prepared to answer questions honestly and frankly. The manager of a certain bank was fond of asking applicants if they knew what their chief faults and virtues were. Most of the applicants were unable to answer this question. Then the manager would ask them if they ever reflected on their own character. Evidently he believed in the motto of the ancient Greeks—"Know thyself." He probably went on the assumption that the person who could answer his two simple questions possessed the integrity and desire for self-improvement that would make him valuable addition to his staff.

In applying for a job, it is wise to take into consideration the character of the interviewer and to adjust oneself to him. If he is quiet and serious, it is best to match one's mood to his. On the other hand, if he is robust[4] and jovial,[5] he will probably expect the applicant to display a little spirit.[6] Some interviewers delight in teasing prospective employees. One of the surest signs of a well-developed personality is the ability to take a joke. In such cases, a little humor on the part of the applicant would not be out of place. He must keep in mind that the interviewer, as an employer, has certain prerogatives.[7]

4 robust 원기 있는, 건장한
5 jovial: cheerful
6 to display a little spirit 약간의 원기를 보이다
7 prerogatives: privileges

14-2.

The Great Stone Face

—Nathaniel Hawthorne

One afternoon, when the sun was going down, a mother and her little boy sat at the door of their cottage, talking about the Great Stone Face. They had but to lift their eyes, and there it was plainly to be seen, though miles away, with the sunshine brightening all its features.

The Great Stone Face was a work of Nature in her mood of majestic playfulness,[1] formed on the perpendicular side of the mountain by some immense rocks, which had been thrown together in such a position as, when viewed at a proper distance, precisely to resemble the features of the human countenance. It seemed as if an enormous giant, or a Titan, had sculptured his own likeness on the precipice. There was the broad arch of the forehead, a hundred feet in height; the nose, with its long bridge; and the vast lips, which, if they could have spoken, would have rolled their thunder accents from one end of the valley to the other.

It was a happy lot[2] for children to grow up to manhood or womanhood

---

1 in her mood of majestic playfulness 자연이 웅대한 장난기에 빠져 만든
2 lot: fortune

with the Great Stone Face before their eyes, for all the features were noble, and the expression was at once grand and sweet, as if it were the glow of a vast, warm heart, that embraced all mankind in its affections, and had room for more. It was an education only to look at it.

As we began with saying, a mother and her little boy sat at their cottage-door, gazing at the Great Stone Face, and talking about it. The child's name was Ernest.[3]

His mother told Ernest a story that her own mother had told to her, when she herself was younger than little Ernest; a story, not of things that were past, but of what was yet to come[4]; a story, nevertheless, so very old that even the Indians, who formerly inhabited this valley, had heard it from their forefathers, to whom, as they affirmed, it had been murmured by the mountain streams, and whispered by the wind among the tree-tops.

The purport was, that, at some future day, a child should be born hereabouts, who was destined to become the greatest and noblest personage of his time, and whose countenance, in manhood, would bear an exact resemblance to the Great Stone Face.

Ernest never forget the story that his mother told him. It was always in his mind, whenever he looked upon the Great Stone Face. He spent his childhood in the log-cottage where he was born, and was dutiful to his mother, and helpful to her in many things, assisting her much with his little hands, and more with his loving heart.

In this manner, from a happy yet often pensive[5] child, he grew up to be

---

3 Ernest 진실한 사람이란 뜻
4 what was yet to come 앞으로 일어날 일
5 pensive 생각에 잠긴

a mild, quiet, unobtrusive[6] boy, and sun-browned with labor in the fields, but with more intelligence brightening his aspect than is seen in many lads who have been taught at famous schools.

About this time, there went a rumor throughout the valley, that the great man, foretold from ages long ago, who was to bear a resemblance to the Great Stone Face, had appeared at last.

It seems that, many years before, a young man had migrated from the valley and settled at a distant seaport, where, after getting together a little money, he had set up as a shopkeeper.

His name—but I could never learn whether it was his real one, or a nickname that had grown out of his habits and success in life—was Gathergold. Being shrewd and active, and endowed by Providence with that inscrutable[7] faculty which develops itself in what the world calls luck, he became an exceedingly rich merchant, and owner of a whole fleet of bulky-bottomed ships. All the countries of the globe appeared to join hands for the mere purpose of adding heap after heap to the mountainous accumulation of this one man's wealth.

When Mr. Gathergold had become so very rich that it would have taken him a hundred years only to count his wealth, he bethought himself of his native valley, and resolved to go back thither, and end his days where he was born. With this purpose in view, he sent a skillful architect to build him such a palace as should be fit for a man of his vast wealth to live in.

In due time, the mansion was finished; next came the upholsterers[8] with

6 unobtrusive: polite
7 inscrutable: mysterious
8 upholsterers 소파 등에 덮개를 씌우는 일을 하는 사람들, 가구상인

magnificent furniture; then, a whole troop of black and white servants, the harbingers[9] of Mr. Gathergold, who, in his own majestic person, was expected to arrive at sunset. Our friend Ernest, meanwhile, had been deeply stirred by the idea that the great man, the noble man, the man of prophecy, after so many ages of delay, was at length to be made manifest to his native valley. He knew, boy as he was, that there were a thousand ways in which Mr. Gathergold, with his vast wealth, might transform himself into an angel of beneficence, and assume a control over human affairs as wide and benignant[10] as the smile of the Great Stone Face. Full of faith and hope, Ernest doubted not that what the people said was true, and that now he was to behold the living likeness of those wondrous features on the mountain-side.

While the boy was still gazing up the valley, and fancying, as he always did, that the Great Stone Face returned his gaze and looked kindly at him, the rumbling of wheels was heard, approaching swiftly along the winding road.

"Here he comes!" cried a group of people who were assembled to witness the arrival.

"Here he comes the great Mr. Gathergold!"

A carriage, drawn by four horses, dashed round the turn of the road. Within it, thrust partly out of the window, appeared the physiognomy[11] of a little old man, with a skin as yellow as if his own Midas-hand had transmuted[12] it. He had a low forehead, small, sharp eyes, puckered about with[13] innumerable wrinkles, and very thin lips, which he made still thinner by

9 harbingers 선구자, 선발자
10 benignant[binignənt] 정이 깊은
11 physiognomy: face
12 transmuted: changed
13 puckered about with ~로 주름이 졌다.

pressing them forcibly together.

"The very image of the Great Stone Face!" shouted the people. "Sure enough, the old prophecy is true; and here we have the great man come, at last!"

And, what greatly perplexed Ernest, they seemed actually to believe that here was the likeness which they spoke of. By the roadside there chanced to be an old beggar-woman and two little beggar-children, stragglers[14] from some far-off region, who, as the carriage rolled onward, held out their hands and lifted up their doleful[15] voices, most piteously beseeching[16] charity.

A yellow claw—the very same that had clawed together so much wealth—poked[17] itself out of the coach-window, and dropped some copper coins upon the ground; so that, though the great man's name seems to have been Gathergold, he might just as suitably have been nicknamed Scattercopper. Still, nevertheless, with an earnest shout, and evidently with as much good faith as ever, the people bellowed,[18]—"He is the very image of the Great Stone Face!"

But Ernest turned sadly from the wrinkles shrewdness of that sordid visage,[19] and gazed up the valley, where, amid a gathering mist, gilded by the last sunbeams, he could still distinguish those glorious features which had impressed themselves into his soul. Their aspect cheered him. What did the benign lips seem to say? "He will come! Fear not, Ernest; the man will come!"

The years went on, and Ernest ceased to be a boy. He had grown to be a young man now. He attracted little notice from the other inhabitants of the

---

14 stragglers 부랑자들
15 doleful: sorrowful, sad
16 beseeching: asking
17 poked (노란 갈고리 같은 손을) 쑥 내밀고
18 bellowed: cried, shouted
19 sordid visage 지저분한 얼굴

valley; for they saw nothing remarkable in his way of life, save that, when the labor of the day was over, he still loved to go apart and gaze and meditate upon the Great Stone Face. According to their idea of the matter, it was a folly, indeed, but pardonable, inasmuch as Ernest was industrious, kind, and neighborly, and neglected no duty for the sake of indulging this idle habit.

They knew not that the Great Stone Face had become a teacher to him, and that the sentiment which was expressed in it would enlarge the young man's heart, and fill it with wider and deeper sympathies than other hearts. They knew not that thence would come a better wisdom than could be learned from books, and a better life than could be molded on the defaced example of other human lives. Neither did Ernest know that the thoughts and affections which came to him so naturally, in the fields and at the fireside, and wherever he communed with himself were of a higher tone than those which all men shared with him. A simple soul, — simple as when his mother first taught him the old prophecy, — he beheld the marvelous features beaming adown[20] the valley, and still wondered that their human counterpart[21] was so long in making his appearance.

It so happened that a native-born son of the valley, many years before, had enlisted as a soldier, and, after a great deal of hard fighting, had now become an illustrious commander. Whatever he maybe called in history, he was known in camps and on the battlefield under the nickname of Old Blood-an-Thunder.[22] This war-worn veteran, being now infirm with age and wounds,[23] and weary of the turmoil[24] of a military life, and of the roll of the

---

20 adown: downward

21 their human counterpart 그 얼굴 모습과 꼭 닮은 사람

22 Old Blood-an-Thunder 노인 유혈장군

23 being now infirm with age and wounds 나이와 싸움터에서 입은 상처로 몸이 쇠약해지고

24 turmoil 혼란; 시끄러움; 격무

drum and the clangor of the trumpet,[25] that had so long been ringing in his ears, had lately signified[26] a purpose of returning to his native valley, hoping to find repose where he remembered to have left it.[27]

The inhabitants, his old neighbors and their grown-up children, were resolved to welcome the renowned warrior with a salute of cannon and a public dinner; and all the more enthusiastically, it being affirmed that now, at last, the likeness of the Great Stone Face had actually appeared. An aid-de-camp[28] of Old Blood-an-Thunder, traveling through the valley, was said to have been struck with the resemblance.

It is true, Ernest had imagined that this long-looked-for personage would appear in the character of a man of peace, uttering wisdom, and doing good, and making people happy. But, taking an habitual breadth of view,[29] with all his simplicity, he contended that Providence should choose its own method of blessing mankind, and could conceive that this great end[30] might be effected even by a warrior and a bloody sword, should inscrutable wisdom see fit to order matters so.[31]

"The general! The general!" was now the cry. "Hush! silence! Old Blood-an- Thunder's going to make a speech."

Even so; for, the cloth being removed, the general's health had been drunk

---

25 [weary] of the roll of the drum and the clangor of the trumpet 계속적인 북소리와 나팔소리에도 싫증이 나

26 had lately signified 최근에 밝혔다

27 hoping to find repose where he remembered to have left it 예전에 버리고 온 평온을 그곳에서 되찾을 생각이라고

28 aid-de-camp 전속부관

29 taking an habitual breadth of view 언제나처럼 폭넓은 견해를 취하면서

30 end는 purpose

31 should inscrutable wisdom see fit to order matters so 만약 헤아릴 수 없는 지혜가 일을 그런 식으로 하게 하는 것[그렇게 순서를 잡는 것]이 적당하다고 본다면. see fit to do ~하는 것이 적당하다고 본다.

amid shouts of applause,[32] and he now stood upon his feet to thank the company. Ernest saw him. And there, too, visible in the same glance, through the vista of the forest, appeared the Great Stone Face! And was there, indeed, such a resemblance as the crowd had testified?

Alas, Ernest could not recognize it! He beheld a war-worn and weather-beaten countenance, full of energy, and expressive of an iron will; but the gentle wisdom, the deep, broad, tender sympathies, were altogether wanting in[33] Old Blood-an-Thunder's visage; and even if the Great Stone Face had assumed his look of stern command, the milder traits would still have tempered it.

"This is not the man of prophecy," sighed Ernest to himself, as he made his way out of the throng. "And must the world wait longer yet?"

More years sped swiftly and tranquilly away. Ernest still dwelt in his native valley, and was now a man of middle age. By imperceptible degrees, he had become known among the people. Now, as heretofore, he labored for his bread, and was the same simple-hearted man that he had always been. But he had thought and felt so much, he had given so many of the best hours of his life to unworldly hopes for some great good to mankind, that it seemed as though he had been talking with the angels, and had imbibed[34] a portion of their wisdom unawares. It was visible in the calm and well-considered beneficience of his daily life, the quiet stream of which had made a wide green margin all along its course.[35]

Not a day passed by, that the world was not the better because[36] this

---

32 the general's health had been drunk amid shouts of applause 건강을 축하하는 갈채 속에 건배가 이루어지자

33 were altogether wanting in ~에는 전혀 없다.

34 imbibed 받아들였다

35 made a wide green margin all along its course 강기슭으로 짙푸른 녹색 물결을 보내며

36 Not a day passed by, that the world was not the better because~ ~때문에 세상은 하루하루 그만큼

man, humble as he was, had lived. He never stepped aside from his own path, yet would always reach a blessing to his neighbor. Almost involuntarily, too, he had become a preacher. The pure and high simplicity of his thought, which, as one of its manifestations, took shape in the good deeds that dropped silently from his hand, flowed also forth in speech. He uttered truths that wrought[37] and molded the lives of those who heard him.

When the people's minds had a little time to cool, they were ready enough to acknowledge their mistake in imagining a similarity between General Blood-and- Thunder's truculent[38] physiognomy and the benign visage on the mountain-side. But now, again, there were reports and many paragraphs in the newspapers, affirming that the likeness of the Great Stone Face had appeared upon the broad shoulders of a certain eminent statesman.

He, like Mr. Gathergold and Old Blood-and-Thunder, was a native of the valley, but had left it in his early days,[39] and taken up the trades of law and politics. Instead of the rich man's wealth and the warrior's sword, he had but a tongue, and it was mightier than both together. So wonderfully eloquent was he, that whatever he might choose to say, his auditors had no choice but to believe him; wrong looked like right, and right like wrong; for when it pleased him,[40] he could make a kind of illuminated fog with his mere breath, and obscure the natural daylight with it. His tongue, indeed, was a magic instrument: sometimes it rumbled like the thunder; sometimes it warbled[41] like

좋아졌다.

37 work의 과거로 만들다; 세공하다의 뜻이고, work upon 작용하다, 영향을 주다라는 뜻으로 쓰인다.

38 truculent 야만스런; 무서운; 호전적인

39 in his early days: when he was young

40 for when it pleased him 그럴 마음만 먹으면

41 warble 지껄이다

the sweetest music. It was the blast of war,[42]—the song of peace; and it seemed to have a heart in it, when there was no such matter.[43] In good truth,[44] he was a wondrous man; and when his tongue had acquired him all other imaginable success,—when it had been heard in halls of state,[45] and in the courts of princes and potentates,[46]—after it had made him known all over the world, even as a voice crying from shore to shore,—it finally persuaded his countrymen[47] to select him for the Presidency.

Before this time,—indeed, as soon as he began to grow celebrated,—his admirers had found out the resemblance between him and the Great Stone Face; and so much were they struck by it, that throughout the country this distinguished gentleman was known by the name of Old Stony Phiz. The phrase was considered as giving a highly favorable aspect to his political prospects; for, as is likewise the case with the Popedom,[48] nobody ever becomes president without taking a name other his own.

While his friends[49] were doing their best to make President, Old Stony Phiz, as he was called, set out on a visit to the valley where he was born. Of course, he had no other object than to shake hands with his fellow-citizens, and neither thought nor cared about any effect which his progress through the country might have upon the election. Magnificent preparations were made to receive the illustrious statesman, a cavalcade[50] of horsemen set forth to meet

---

42 the blast of war 싸움터의 폭음
43 when there was no such matter 그럴 마음이 없을 때도
44 In good truth: Certainly, Indeed
45 halls of state 주 의사당
46 potentates 권력자들
47 countrymen 동[고]향 사람들
48 Popedom 로마교황
49 friends: followers
50 cavalcade 기마행진

him at the boundary line of the State, and all the people left their business and gathered along the wayside to see him pass. Among these was Ernest.

All this while the people were throwing up their hats and shouting, with enthusiasm so contagious that the heart of Ernest kindled up, and he likewise threw up his hat, and shouted, as loudly as the loudest, "Huzza for the great man! Huzza for Old Stony Phiz!" But as yet he had not seen him.

"Here he is, now!" cried those who stood near Ernest. "There! There! Look at Old Stony Phiz and then at the Old Man of the Mountain, and see if they are not as like as two twin brothers!"

In the midst of all this gallant array,[51] came an open barouche,[52] drawn by four white horses; and in the barouche, with his massive head uncovered, sat the illustrious statesman, Old Stony Phiz himself.

"Confess it," said one of Ernest's neighbors to him; "the Great Stone Face has met its match at last!"

Now, it must be owned that, at his first glimpse of the countenance which was bowing and smiling from the barouche, Ernest did fancy that there was a resemblance between it and the old familiar face upon the mountain-side. The brow, with its massive depths and loftiness, and all the other features, indeed, were boldly and strongly hewn,[53] as if in emulation of[54] a more than heroic, of a Titanic model. But the sublimity and stateliness, the grand expression of a divine sympathy, that illuminated the mountain visage, and etherealized[55] its ponderous granite substance[56] into spirit, might here be sought in vain.

---

51 gallant array 화려한 모임

52 open barouche[bərúːʃ] 뚜껑 없는 대형 사륜마차

53 hew의 p, pp. 뜻은 cut, carve

54 in emulation of ~를 모방하여

55 etherealized 영성화(靈性化)했다, 영기를 불어넣다.

56 ponderous granite substance 장중한 바윗덩어리

Something had been originally left out, or had departed. And therefore the marvelously gifted statesman had always a weary gloom in the deep caverns of his eyes, as of a child that has outgrown its playthings, or a man of mighty faculties and little aims, whose life, with all its high performance, was vague and empty, because no high purpose had endowed it with reality.

Still, Ernest's neighbor was thrusting his elbow into his side, and pressing him for an answer.

"Confess! confess! is not he the very picture of your Old Man of the Mountain?"

"No!" said Ernest, bluntly, "I see little or no likeness."

The years hurried onward, treading in their haste on one another's heels.[57] And now they began to bring white hairs, and scatter them over the head of Ernest; they made reverend wrinkles across his forehead, and furrows in his cheeks. He was an aged man. But not in vain had he grown old; more than the white hairs on his head were the sage thoughts in his mind; his wrinkles and furrows were inscriptions[58] that Time had graved,[59] and in which he had written legends of wisdom that had been tested by the tenor of a life.[60] And Ernest had ceased[61] to be obscure.[62]

Unsought for, undesired, had come the fame which so many seek, and made him known in the great world, beyond the limits of the valley in which he had dwelt so quietly. College professors, and even the active men of cities, came from far to see and converse with Ernest; for the report had gone abroad

---

57 tread on a person's heels ~을 바짝 뒤따르다
58 inscriptions 명각, 비문
59 graved: buried
60 the tenor of a life: the course through life 인생의 행로
61 ceased: stopped
62 obscure: unclear

that this simple husbandman[63] had ideas unlike those of other men, not gained from books, but of a higher tone, — a tranquil and familiar majesty, as if he had been talking with the angels as his daily friends.

Whether it were sage, statesman, or philanthropist, Ernest received these visitors with the gentle sincerity that had characterized him from boyhood, and spoke freely with them of whatever came uppermost,[64] or lay deepest in his heart or their own. while they talked together, his face would kindle, unawares, and shine upon them, as with a mild evening light. Pensive[65] with the fullness of such discourse, his guests took leave and went their way; and passing up the valley, paused to look at the Great Stone Face, imagining that they had seen its likeness in a human countenance, but could not remember where.

While Ernest had been growing up and growing old, a bountiful[66] Providence[67] had granted a new poet to this earth. He, likewise, was a native of the valley, but had spent the greater part of his life at a distance from that romantic region, pouring out his sweet music amid the bustle and din[68] of cities. Often, however, did the mountains which had been familiar to him in his childhood lift their snowy peaks into the clear atmosphere of his poetry. Neither was the Great Stone Face forgotten, for the poet had celebrated it in an ode,[69] which was grand enough to have been uttered[70] by its own majestic lips.

This man of genius, we may say, had come down from heaven with

---

63 husbandman: farmer
64 of whatever came uppermost 우선 화제에 오른 것에 대해
65 pensive: thoughtful
66 bountiful: generous 관대한, 물건을 아끼지 않는
67 Providence (하느님의) 섭리
68 bustle and din 혼잡과 소음
69 ode[oud] 송시: 특정한 사람이나 사물을 읊은 고상한 서정시
70 utter: tell, say

wonderful endowments[71]. If he sang of a mountain, the eyes of all mankind beheld a mightier grandeur reposing on its breast,[72] or soaring to it summit, than had before been seen there. If his theme were a lovely lake, a celestial smile had now been thrown over it, to gleam forever on its surface. If it were the vast old sea, even the deep immensity of its dread bosom[73] seemed to swell the higher, as if moved by the emotions of the song.

The songs of this poet found their way to Ernest. He read them after his customary toil, seated on the bench before his cottage-door, where for such a length of time he had filled his repose with thought, by gazing at the Great Stone Face. And now as he read stanzas that caused the soul to thrill within him, he lifted his eyes to the vast countenance beaming on him so benignantly.

"O majestic friend," he murmured, addressing[74] the Great Stone Face, "is not this man[75] worthy to resemble thee?"

The Face seemed to smile, but answered not a word.

Now it happened that the poet, though he dwelt so far away, had not only heard of Ernest, but had meditated much upon his character, until he deemed[76] nothing so desirable as to meet this man, whose untaught wisdom walked hand in hand with the noble simplicity of his life.

One summer morning, therefore, he took passage by the railroad, and, in the decline of the afternoon, alighted from the cars at no great distance from Ernest's cottage. The great hotel, which had formerly been the palace, of Mr. Gathergold was close at hand, but the poet, with his carpet-bag on his arm,

---

71 endowments 천부적인 재능

72 reposing on its breast 산의 가슴에 깃들고

73 even the deep immensity of its dread bosom 그 무서운 바다 한복판에 숨겨진 깊은 무한함조차

74 addressing ~에 호소하면서

75 this man은 the poet

76 deemed: thought

inquired at once where Ernest dwelt, and was resolved to be accepted as his guest.

Approaching the door, he there found the good old man, holding a volume in his hand, which alternately he read, and then with a finger between the leaves, looked lovingly at the Great Stone Face.

"Good evening," said the poet. "Can you give a traveler a night's lodging?"

"Willingly," answered Ernest; and then he added, smiling, "Methinks I never saw the Great Stone Face look so hospitably at a stranger."

The poet sat down on the bench beside him, and he and Ernest talked together. Often he had the poet held intercourse with[77] the wittiest and the wisest, but never before with man like Ernest, whose thoughts and feelings gushed up[78] with such a natural freedom, and who made great truths so familiar by his simple utterance of them. Angels, as had been so often said, seemed to have wrought[79] with him at his labor in the fields; angels seemed to have sat with him by the fireside; and, dwelling with angels as friend with friends, he had imbibed[80] the sublimity of their ideas, and imbued it with[81] the sweet and lowly charm of household words. So thought the poet.

And Ernest, on the other hand, was moved and agitated[82] by the living images which the poet flung out of his mind, and which peopled[83] all the air about the cottage-door with shapes of beauty, both gay and pensive. The sympathies of these two men instructed them with a profounder sense than

---

77 held intercourse with ~와 교제하고 있었다.
78 gush up 분출하다, 솟아나오다.
79 wrought: worked
80 imbibed 마시다, 흡수하다
81 imbued it with~ 그것에 ~를 불어 넣다(스며들게 하다)
82 agitated: excited
83 peopled: filled with people

either could have attained alone. Their minds accorded into one strain,[84] and made delightful music which neither of them could have claimed as all his own, nor distinguished his own share from the other's. They led one another, as it were, into a high pavilion[85] of their thoughts, so remote, and hitherto so dim, that they had never entered it before, and so beautiful that they desired to be there always.

As Ernest listened to the poet, he imagined that the Great Stone Face was bending forward to listen too. He gazed earnestly into the poet's glowing eyes.

"Who are you, my strangely gifted guest? he said.

The poet laid his finger on the volume that Ernest had been reading.

"You have read these poems," said he. "You know me, then—for I wrote them."

Again, and still more earnestly than before, Ernest examined the poet's features; then turned toward the Great Stone Face; then back, with an uncertain aspect, to his guest. But his countenance fell; he shook his head, and signed.

"Wherefore[86] are you sad?" inquired the poet.

"Because," replied Ernest, "all through life I have awaited the fulfillment of a prophecy; and, when I read these poems, I hoped that it might be fulfilled in you."

"You hoped," answered the poet, faintly smiling, "to find in me the likeness of the Great Stone Face. And you are disappointed, as formerly with Mr. Gathergold, and Old Blood-and-Thunder, and Old Stony Phiz. Yes,

---

84 strain 기질, 경향
85 pavilion 정자, 누각
86 Wherefore: For what reason, Why

Ernest, it is my doom.[87] You must add my name to the illustrious three,[88] and record another failure of your hopes. For—in shame and sadness do I speak it, Ernest—I am not worthy to be typifies by yonder benign and majestic image."

"And why?" asked Ernest. He pointed to the volume. "Are not those thoughts divine?"

"They have a strain[89] of the Divinity," replied the poet. "You can hear in them the far-off echo of a heavenly song. But my life, dear Ernest, has not corresponded with my thought. I have had grand dreams, but they have been only dreams because I have lived—and that, too, by my own choice—among poor and mean realities. Sometimes even—shall I dare to say it?—I lack faith in the grandeur, the beauty, and the goodness, which my own works are said to have made more evident in nature and in human life. Why, then, pure seeker of the good and true, shouldst thou hope to find me in yonder image of the divine?"

Ernest began to speak, giving to the people of what was in his heart and mind. His words had power, because they accorded with his thoughts; and his thoughts had reality and depth, because they harmonized with the life which he had always lived. It was not mere breath that this preacher uttered; they were the words of life, because a life of good deeds and holy love was melted into them. Pearls, pure and rich, had been dissolved into this precious draught.[90]

The poet, as he listened, felt that the being and character of Ernest were a nobler strain of poetry than he had ever written. His eyes glistening with tears, he gazed reverentially at the venerable man, and said within himself that

---

87 doom: fate
88 the illustrious three: the famous three figures
89 strain 가락
90 draught = draft 한 모금의 물, 물약

never was there an aspect so worthy of a prophet and a sage as that mild, sweet, thoughtful countenance, with the glory of white hair diffused about it.

At a distance, but distinctly to be seen, high up in the golden light of the setting sun, appeared the Great Stone Face, with hoary[91] mists around it, like the white hairs around the brow of Ernest. Its look of grand beneficience seemed to embrace the world.

At that moment, in sympathy with a thought which he was about to utter, the face of Ernest assumed a grandeur of expression, so imbued with[92] benevolence, that the poet, by an irresistible impulse, threw his arms aloft, and shouted, — "Behold! Behold! Ernest is himself the likeness of the Great Stone Face!"

Then all the people looked, and saw that what the deep-sighted[93] poet said was true. The prophecy was fulfilled. But Ernest, having finished what he had to say, took the poet's arm, and walked slowly homeward, still hoping that some wiser and better man than himself would by and by appear, bearing a resemblance to the Great Stone Face.

> The human face is the masterpiece of God. The eyes reveal the soul, the mouth the flesh. The chin stands for purpose, the nose means will; But over and behind all is that fleeting something we call "expression."
>
> — Elbert Hubbard, *Little Journeys to the Homes of Good Men and Great*

91 hoary 회백색의

92 imbue with 감화시키다, 불어넣다, 스며들게 하다

93 deep-sighted: far-sighted 선견지명이 있는

Pattern Usage

1. You've got to keep your nose to the grindstone.[94] You won't mind that, will you?
2. How much salary do you expect? I'd rather leave that to you, Boss.
3. Above all, be careful not to leave the gas turned on.
4. For people who are overweight, they prefer the misery of excess weight to the cure of dieting.
   The most obvious cure for their illness is to simply cut down on their food.
   If you'd cut down on your recreation and devote more time to your studies, you'd get better marks in school.
   If I cut down on my smoking, I can save twenty thousand won a month.

Comprehension Check-up

1. What do we know the naming of the characters such as Ernest, Gathergold, Old Blood-and-Thunder, Old Stony Phiz, etc.? Consider these words, earnestly.

2. What does imply that a person tries to resemble a great figure?

94 have got to keep your nose to the grindstone 언제나 일하지 않으면 안 된다.

Grammatical Tips

● **가정법(Subjunctive Mood)**

1. 직설법과 가정법의 관계

(a) 직설법 As I **am** a student (now), I **can't** propose marriage to Mary (now).

(b) 가정법 If I **were not** a student (now), I **could** propose marriage to Mary (now).

* ① 가정법은 직설법보다 앞선 시제
  ② 내용은 반대, 즉 긍정은 부정으로, 부정은 긍정으로 바꾼다.
  ③ 가정법 과거의 시제는 현재이며, 가정법 과거완료는 과거시제다.

2. 가정법 현재: 현재 또는 미래에 대한 불확실한 상상, 사실이나 의심을 표현할 때 사용한다.

(a) If it be(is) rainy tomorrow, I will not go to church.
If you mix yellow and blue, you get green.

(b) (기원문) (May) God save the king! God bless you!

(c) (주장, 명령, 제안, 충고, 요구, 필요, 당연) that 절은 가정법 현재이며 that clause의 (should)는 보통 생략한다.

* insist, ask, order, desire, suggest, wonder, request, require, propose, demand that 주어 (should) 동사
* 동사 the command, instructions, suggestion, request, pressure that 주어 (should) 동사
* be imperative, essential, necessary, advisable, of no importance, suggestive, etc. that 주어 (should) 동사

3. 가정법 과거

(a) If 주어 **과거동사**, 주어 **would** (또는 should, could, might) 동사.
  * If I **had** much money (now), I **would** buy the book (now).

(= As I don't have much money (now), I can't buy the book (now).

(b) It is (high 또는 about) **time** (that) 주어 should 동사 (또는 과거동사).

It is time I went back to my house.

(c) 주어 **would** (또는 had) **rather** (that) 주어 과거동사

I would rather you went to your home.

(d) 주어 **had better** 동사

You had better see a doctor. (= It would be better for you to see a doctor.)

(e) He is, as it were, a sleeping lion.

4. 가정법 과거완료

If 주어 **had 과거분사**, 주어 **would** (또는 should, could, might) **have 과거분사**.

If I had had much money, I would have bought a luxury car.

(= As I didn't have much money, I couldn't buy a luxury car.)

5. 가정법 미래: 현재나 미래에 대해 불확실한 것, 또 가능성이 희박한 일을 가정하거나 미래에 대한 의구심을 나타낼 때 사용한다.

(a) If 주어 should 동사, 주어 would(should, will, shall, must) 동사: 막연한 가정

If he should come, I will tell you.

If you should fail, what would you do?

(b) If 주어 would 동사, 주어 would(should, shall, will, must) 동사: 소망이나 의지

If you would write a novel, you must read many books.

(c) If 주어 were to 동사, 주어 would(should, could, might) 동사: 불가능한 일을 가정

If the sun were to rise in the west, I would not change my mind.

6. 혼합가정법(가정법 혼합시제): 보통 과거의 사실이 현재에 영향을 줄 때 사용한다.

If he had not been killed in Vietnam War, he would be 65 now.

If you had listened to my advice, you would not be in danger.

(If절은 가정법 과거완료, 주절은 가정법 과거)

7. if 대용구

Unless he were honest, I would not employ him.

Even if (Even though) I were ill, I would go there.

I would have forgiven him, **provided** (that) he had acknowledged his falut.

Assuming (that) he should know the secret, we would be ruined.

In case (that) it should rain, the plan would fail.

Suppose (Supposing that) he were to become President, his father would be much delighted.

But for (Without) water, we couldn't live any more.

(= Were it not for water, we couldn't live any more.

Exercise

* Distinguish the following word, 'lot,' in each context.

a lot of
parking lot
It was a lot for me to escape the disaster.

* Read the following passage and answer the questions.

"One of seventeen children of a Boston soap and a candle maker, Benjamin Franklin had left home as a boy after receiving barely two years of schooling and established himself as a printer in Philadelphia. By dint of[95] hard work and steady application he had made himself into one of the most respected thinkers and wealthiest businessmen in the colonies. His experiments with electricity, unfairly diminished in the popular mind to inventing the lightening rod and nearly killing himself by foolishly flying a kite in a thunderstorm, were among the most exciting scientific achievements of the eighteenth century and made him one of the celebrated scientists of the day (though he was never called a *scientist* in his lifetime, the word not being coined until 1840; in the 1700s, scientists were *natural philosophers*). The terms he created in the course of his experiments—*battery*, *armature*, *positive*, *negative*, and *condenser*, among others[96]—show that he was a good deal more than a mildly quizzical fellow who just wanted to see what would happen if he nudged[97] a kite into some storm clouds.

His life was one of relentless industry. He invented countless useful objects, and helped to found America's first volunteer fire department, its first fire insurance company (the Hand-in-Hand), one of Philadelphia's first libraries, and the respected if somewhat

---

95 by dint of ~의 덕으로, ~에 의하여
96 Bill Bryson, *Made in America*, New York: William Morrow and Co., Inc., 1994. p.50에서 재인용
97 nudge 찌르다, 움직이다

overnamed American Philosophical Society for the Promotion of Useful Knowledge to be Held at Philadelphia. He created an eternal literary character, the Richard of *Poor Richard's Almanack*, filled the world with maxims and *bons mots*,[98] corresponded endlessly with the leading minds of Europe and America, wrote essays on everything from how to select a mistress (take an older woman) to how to avoid flatulance[99] (drink perfume), and in 1737 drew up the first list of American slang terms for drunkenness. He represented America overseas with intelligence and skill and, of course, was one of the shapers of the Declaration of Independence" (Bryson 50–51).

America had a long tradition of productive tinkering. Jefferson invented plow, which secured him a *prix d'honneur* from a French agricultural academy (though in fact it didn't work very well), and filled Monticello with self-invented contrivances designed to thwart small everyday irritants. Franklin, as everyone knows, was a manic inventor. He gave the world bifocals, the lightening rod, extendable grippers for taking items off high shelves, possibly the rocking chair, and certainly the Franklin stove (though for its first forty years it was more generally known as the *Pennsylvania fireplace*)—and always, always with a practical bent. "What signifies philosophy that does not apply to some use?" he asked. Like Jefferson, he never profited from any of them (86–87).

It was at Jefferson's insistence that the U.S. Patent Office was set up in 1790. Even Abraham Lincoln found time to take out a patent (No. 6469: A Device for Buoying Vessels over Shoals).

1. What had made Benjamin Franklin into a great thinker and wealthy businessman?
   a. Because he had many brothers and sisters
   b. Because he established himself as a printer in Philadelphia
   c. By dint of hard work and steady application
   d. By his experiments with electricity

2. What did he invent, relating to electricity?

98 *bon mot* [banmou] (F) 명언, 명문구
99 flatulance 위장에 가스가 참; 허세, 허영; 거만

3. What did he do foolishly?

4. What did they call scientists in the 1700s in the colonies?

* Leader or Follower

1. Are you usually the first of your friends to try new things?
2. Do you ignore what's trendy or have some interest to buy popular things?
3. Are you confident in your potential talents and future?
4. Are you nervous making difficult decisions?
5. Do you get excited by new challenges?
6. Are you someone that others see as a role model?

Unit 15

15-1. *The Mobility of Americans*

15-2. *American Inventions*

15-3. *Travel*

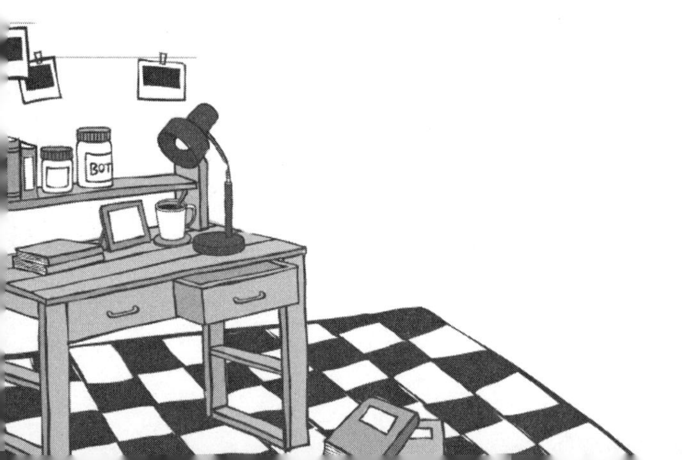

15-1.

The Mobility of Americans

Americans have a long history of moving about. Their ancestors all migrated from somewhere else not too many generations ago. These ancestors were people who were willing to take frightful risks with the aim of improving their lot;[1] for shipwrecks,[2] hunger, disease, Indian raids, and loneliness were regular dangers in settling the new land.

For three hundred years the story of America was one of picking up the household[3] and moving farther west. Those who came first settled along the Atlantic coast; then crossed the Appalachian Mountains.[4] The thirteen original colonies needed more land. The most notable expansion of the country occurred

---

1 lot에는 다양한 뜻이 있다. 여기서는 다음 중 세 번째에 해당되며 운명이라는 뜻이다.
1. a large number or amount or extent
2. a parcel of land having fixed boundaries ex) a parking lot
3. one's overall circumstance or condition in life
4. anything taken or chosen at random
5. (Old Testament) nephew of Abraham; God destroyed Sodom and Gomorrah but chose to spare Lot and his family who were told to flee without looking back at the destruction.

2 shipwrecks 파멸, 실패 an irretrievable loss

3 picking up the household: gathering the household goods

4 Appalachian Mountains: mountain system in eastern North America, extending from South Quebec to north Alabama

in 1803, when the United States purchased the Louisiana territory from France. Later, having made treaties with Mexico and England, the United States obtained land reaching to the Pacific Ocean. Especially during the 1800's the settlers were moving all the time. First, trappers[5] and scouts would go on horseback. A generation later came mining prospectors[6] in wagon trains,[7] and still later in covered wagons came farmers and their families who wanted to settle the land.

The rapidity with which the country has been settled and the fact that the people move about great deal have been the main factors contributing to the uniformity in American life—as is seen in the same main streets with the same chain stores from coast to coast, the same type of school system and other things.

---

5 trappers: people who trap animals, especially, fur-bearing animals
6 mining prospectors: people who searches for a mineral deposit
7 wagon trains: long lines of moving wagons

15-2.

American Inventions

Charles Goodyear personified most of the qualities of the classic American inventor—total belief in the product, years of sacrifice, blind devotion to an idea—but with one engaging difference: he didn't have the faintest idea what he was doing. Described by one biographer as a "gentle lunatic," Goodyear in 1834 became fascinated with rubber. It was a wonderfully promising material—pliant, waterproof, rugged, and durable[1]—but it had many intractable[2] shortcomings. For one thing, it had a low melting point. Boots made of rubber were fine in winter, but at the first sign of warm weather they would gooily[3] decompose[4] and quickly begin to stink.

Goodyear decided to make it his life's work to solve these problems. To say that he became obsessed only begins to hint at the degree of his commitment. Over the next nine years, he sold or pawned everything he owned,

1 pliant(pliable), waterproof, rugged[rʌgid] (1. 우툴두툴한 2. 단단한, 억센) and durable 유연하고 물이 새지 않고 단단하면서 오래가는

2 intractable 처리하기 힘든, 다루기 어려운

3 gooily: gooey 부드럽고 끈적거리는

4 decompose 1. 분해시키다. The bacteria decompose the impurities into a gas and solids. 2. decay

raced through his friends' and family's money, occasionally resorted to begging, and generally inflicted[5] loving but untold hardship on his long-suffering wife and numerous children. He turned the family kitchen into a laboratory and, with only the most basic understanding of the chemistry involved, frequently filled the house with noxious gases and at least once nearly asphyxiated[6] himself. Nothing he tried worked. To demonstrate the material's versatility,[7] he took to wearing a suit made entirely of rubber, but this merely underlined its acute malodorousness[8] and its owner's faltering[9] grip on reality. Amazingly, everyone stood by him. His wife did whatever he asked of her, and relatives gladly handed him their fortunes. One brother-in-law parted with $46,000 and never whimpered[10] when all it resulted in was tubs[11] of noisome slop.[12] With implacable[13] resolve,[14] Goodyear churned out[15] one product after another—rubber mailbags, life preservers,[16], boots, rainwear—that proved disastrously ineffective. Even with the lavish[17] support of friends and relatives, Goodyear constantly lived on the edge of penury.[18] In 1840, when his two-year-old son died, the family couldn't even afford a coffin.

---

5 inflicted: gave
6 asphyxiated[æsfiksieitid] 질식시키다 suffocate
7 versatility 다예 다재, 다기능성
8 malodorousness 악취, 나쁜 냄새 cf. mal(bad)+odor[oudər], smell
9 faltering: 1. 비틀거리는, stumbling 2. 멈칫거리는
10 whimper: 1. 훌쩍이다 2. 투덜거리다
11 tub 통. Let everyone tub stand on its own bottom. 사람은 누구나 제 힘으로 살아야 한다.
12 slop 흙탕물, slush
13 implacable 달래기 어려운, 화해할 수 없는; relentless
14 resolve 용해하다. Water maybe resolved into oxygen and hydrogen. n. 결심, 결의
15 churn out 대량 생산하다.
16 life preserver 구명구(구명 재킷)
17 lavish 아낌없는
18 penury[penjəri] 빈곤, destitution; 궁핍

Finally in 1843, entirely by accident, he had his breakthrough.[19] He spilled some India rubber[20] and sulfur on the top of his stove and in so doing discovered the secret of producing a rubber that was waterproof, pliant, and resistant to extremes of heat and cold, made an ideal insulator, didn't break when dropped or struck, and above all, was practically odorless. Goodyear hastily secured a patent and formed the Naugatuck India-Rubber Company. At long last he and his family were poised for[21] the fame and fortune that their years of sacrifice so clearly warranted.

It was not to be. Goodyear's process was so easily duplicated that other manufacturers simply stole it. Even the name by which the process became known, *vulcanization*[22], was coined by an English pirate. He had endless problems protecting his patents. The French gave him a patent but then withdrew it on a technicality, and when he traveled to France to protest the matter, he found himself tossed into a debtors' prison. He made more money from his autobiography than he ever did from his invention. When he died in 1860, he left his family saddled with debts. The company that proudly bears his name, the Goodyear Tire and Rubber Company, had nothing to do with him or his descendants. It was named Goodyear by two brothers in Akron, Ohio, Frank and Charles Seiberling, who simply admired him.

Next, let's consider the fate of poor Elias Howe, a young Boston native who in 1846 produced the first workable sewing machine. So revolutionary was Howe's machine that he couldn't find a clothing mill willing to try it. Depressed

19 breakthrough 돌파구; 타결
20 India rubber 탄성 고무; eraser
21 poise for ~의 준비를 하다. They were poised to conquer the enemy. 그들은 적군을 정복할 태세를 갖추었다.
22 vulcanization 경화(硬化), 가황(加黃)

by his failure, Howe suffered a nervous breakdown[23] and traveled to England, where he hoped his ingenious[24] invention might be given a more congenial[25] reception. It was not. After two years tramping the streets, he was so destitute[26] that he had to work his passage home on a merchant ship. Arriving penniless in Boston, he discovered that in his absence one Isaac Singer had stolen his patent and set up a sewing machine factory and was making money hand over fist.[27] Howe took Singer to court, where two things became clear: Singer was nothing more than a thief, but now an extremely rich one who could afford to hire the sharpest lawyers. After a protracted[28] fight, Singer was eventually compelled to pay Howe a handsome royalty on every machine built. (Having thus secured his fortune, Howe promptly enlisted in the Union Army as a common foot soldier; it was an age of eccentrics[29] as well as of inventors.) Nonetheless, it is Singer's name, not Howe's that is indelibly[30] associated in the popular mind with the sewing machine.

Equally unlucky was J. Murray Spangler, who invented the vacuum cleaner—or *electric suction sweeper*, as he called it—at the turn of the century in New Berlin, Ohio. Unable to make a success of it, he turned for advice to W. H. Hoover, a local leather-goods maker who knew nothing about electrical appliances but did recognize a business opportunity when it fell in his lap. Before long there were Hoover factories all over the world, Hoover was

---

23 a nervous breakdown 신경쇠약
24 ingenious 독창적인, 창의력이 풍부한
25 congenial 1. 마음이 맞는 2. 적합한
26 destitute 1. 빈곤한 2. 결핍한 They are destitute of common sense.
27 hand over fist = hand over hand
28 protract: prolong
29 eccentrics 괴짜, 기인
30 indelibly 지워지지 않게, 영원히

credited with a great invention he had nothing to do with, the British were even turning his name into a verb (to this day they don't vacuum a carpet but hoover it), and J. Murray Spangler was forgotten.

But perhaps the greatest historical snub[31] was that meted out[32] to Professor Joseph Henry of Princeton, who in 1831 invented the telegraph. Henry not only had the idea of transmitting messages as coded electrical impulses[33] via wires, but worked out all the essentials that would be necessary to make such a system feasible.[34] For some reason, though, he never bothered to perfect, or more crucially patent, the process.

That fell to a talented, well-connected, but generally unattractive fellow from Charlestown, Massachusetts, named Samuel Finley Breese Morse. Morse would have been a man of distinction even if he had never perfected the telegraph. His passion was the idea of transmitting messages along wires, to the extent that he abandoned his social career[35] and spent five desperately impoverished years perfecting the telegraph and lobbying Congress for funding. Finally, in 1842, Congress—proving that it is seldom more than half smart—appropriated $30,000 for Morse's wireless experiments and $30,000 to be spent on the equally exciting new science mesmerism.[36]

With his share of funds, Morse strung a wire between Washington and

---

31 snub 타박, 냉대

32 mete out 할당하다, 주다 allot

33 impulse 1. 추진; 충격; 자극 2. 충동; a man of impulse 충동적인 사람 3. 충격 전파, 임펄스

34 feasible 실행할 수 있는, 가능한

35 to the extent that he abandoned his social career 그의 사회적 경력을 포기할 정도로 He was an accomplished artist, a member of Britain's Royal Academy, a professor of fine arts at New York University, a dedicated dabbler in the creative sciences, and a would-be politician of distinctly reactionary bent. He ran twice for mayor of New York on a virulently anti-Catholic ticket and believed, among other things, that slavery was not just a good thing but divinely inspired.

36 mesmerism 최면술 hypnotism

Baltimore and on May 11, 1844, sent the first telegraphic message(it would not be called a *telegram* for another twelve years). The more famous and ringing words, chosen not by Morse but by the daughter of the commissioner of Patents, came at a later public demonstration. Morse's only real invention was the simple code that bears his name.[37] To build a working telegraph, Morse not only stole lavishly from Henry's original papers, but when stuck would call on the eminent scientist for guidance. For years, Henry encouraged and assisted his efforts. Yet later, when Morse had grown immensely famous and rich, he refused to acknowledge even the slightest degree of debt to his mentor.

Within just four years of Morse's first public demonstration, America had five thousand miles of telegraph wire and Morse was widely regarded as the greatest man of his age.

In 1876 came an invention even more useful and lasting, and far more ingenious, than the telegraph—the *telephone*, invented by Alexander Graham Bell and not strictly an American invention, since Bell, a native of Edinburgh, Scotland, didn't become a U.S. citizen until six years later. Bell did not coin the term *telephone*. The word had been around since the 1830s, and had been applied to a number of devices designed to produce noise, from a kind of musical instrument to a particularly insistent foghorn.[38] Bell described his appliance on the patent application as a new kind of "telegraphy" and soon afterward began referring to it as an "electrical speaking telephone." Others commonly referred to it in its early days as a "speaking telegraph."

Bell had become interested in the possibility of long-distance speech

---

37 *SOS*, incidentally, does not stand for *save our ship* or *save our souls*. It stands for nothing. It was chosen as a distress signal at an international conference in 1906 only because its nine keystrokes (three dots, three dashes, three dots) were simple to transmit.

38 foghorn 안개 경적(霧笛)

through his work with the deaf (a misfortune that extended to both his mother and wife). He was just twenty-eight and his assistant, Thomas A. Watson, just twenty-one when they made their breakthrough on March 10, 1876.

Flushed with excitement, Bell and Watson demonstrated their new device to Western Union, but the company's executives—why does this seem so inevitable?—failed to see its potential. "Mr. Bell," they wrote to him, "after careful consideration of your invention, while it is a very interesting novelty, we have come to the conclusion that it has no commercial possibilities," adding that they saw no future for "an electrical toy." Fortunately for Bell, others were not so shortsighted. Within four years of its invention, America had sixty thousand telephones. In the next twenty years that figure would increase to over six million, and Bell's telephone company, renamed American Telephone and Telegraph, would become the largest corporation in America, with stock worth $1,000 a share. The Bell patent became the single most valuable patent in history. The speed with which the telephone insinuated itself into American life is indicated by the fact that by the early 1880s when a person said "I'll call you" it was taken to mean by telephone—or *phone*, as it was already familiarly known. Bell sold his interests[39] in the telephone in 1881 and devoted himself to other scientific pursuits. He invented ailerons[40] for airplanes and made significant contributions to the phonograph,[41] the iron lung,[42] the photoelectric cell,[43] and water desalination.[44]

As the twentieth century dawned, a young graduate of Cornell named

---

39 interest 권리, 소유권, 주식
40 aileron (비행기의) 보조날개
41 phonograph 축음기
42 iron lung 철제 호흡 보조기
43 photoelectric cell 광전지(photoelectrical 광전자(光電子)의)
44 water desalination 담수화. desalinate = desalt 염분을 제거하다

Willis Carrier developed the first modern air conditioner in 1902. Chester Carlson invented xerography[45] in 1942, while the transistor,[46] invented by three researchers at AT&T Bell Laboratories in 1950.

The car was invented in Germany and the radio in Italy, just as radar, the computer, and the jet engine would later be invented in Britain. But where Americans couldn't be touched was in their capacity to exploit[47] new technologies, and no one was better at this than Thomas Alva Edison.

Edison was the archetypal American pragmatist. What he wanted were useful inventions that would make life more agreeable for the user and bring untold wealth to him. With 1,093 patents to his name (though many of these were in fact attributable to his employees), Edison has almost twice as many patents as his nearest contender, Edwin Land (inventor of the Polaroid camera), and no one gave the world a greater range of products that have become central to modern life. He connived[48] against competitors, took personal credit for inventions that were not his, and when all else failed did not hesitate to resort to bribery, slipping New Jersey legislators $1,000 each to produce laws favorable to his interests.

Edison was to be sure a brilliant inventor, with a rare gift for coaxing[49] genius from his employees. But where he truly excelled was as an organizer of systems. The invention of the light bulb was a wondrous thing, but of not much practical use when no one had a socket to plug it into. Edison and his

---

45 xerography[ziragrəfi] 제로그라피, 전자사진

46 A transistor is a semiconductor device used to amplify and switch electronic signals and electrical power. It is composed of semiconductor material with at least three terminals for connection to an external circuit.

47 exploit 개발하다, 활용하다; 이용하다

48 connived 공모하다, 서로 짜다

49 coaxing 어르는, 달래는

tireless workers had to design and build the entire system from scratch, from power stations to cheap and reliable wiring to lamp-stands and switches. The first experimental power plant was built in two semiderelict[50] buildings on Pearl Street in lower Manhattan, and on September 4, 1882, Edison threw a switch that illuminated, if but faintly, eight hundred flicking bulbs all over southern Manhattan. With incredible speed, electric lighting became a wonder of the age. Within months, Edison had set up no fewer than 334 small electrical plants all over the world. Cannily[51] he put them in places where they would be sure to achieve maximum impact: in the New York Stock Exchange, the Palmer House Hotel in Chicago, La Scala opera house in Milan, the dining room of the House of Commons in London. All this made Edison, and America, immensely rich. By 1920 it was estimated that the industries spawned[52] by his inventions and business pursuits—from electric lighting to motion pictures—were worth an aggregate[53] $21.6 billion. No other person did more to make America an economic power.

Edison's other great innovation was the setting up of a laboratory—the "invention factory" in Menro Park, New Jersey—with the express purpose of making technological breakthroughs with commercial potential.[54] Before long, many leading corporations, notably AT&T, General Electric, and Du Pont, were doing the same. Practical science, elsewhere the preserve of academics, had become in America the work of capitalists.

As small companies grew into mighty corporations, a new breed of

---

50 semiderelict[semiderəlikt] 반쯤 버려진

51 cannily 기민하게, 신중히

52 spawn 산란하다, 대량생산하다

53 aggregate vi. n. 집합; 총계

54 with the express purpose of making technological breakthroughs with commercial potential 상업적 가능성으로 기술적인 진전을 이룰 분명한 목적을 가지고

magnates[55] required increasingly grand and imposing headquarters. Fortunately, their need for office space coincided with the development of a radical type of building: the skyscraper. Before 1880s, a building of more than eight or nine stories was impracticable.[56] Such a structure, made of brick, would require so much support as to preclude[57] openings for windows and doors on the lower floors.

Steel frame construction and curtain walling[58] made tall buildings possible, but not necessarily usable. For that, countless secondary innovations were needed, among them the revolving door, without which drafts would be all but uncontrollable, heightening fire risks and making effective heating and cooling an impossibility,[59] and above all, swift, safe passenger elevators.

The elevator was not, as is commonly supposed and even sometimes stated, the invention of Elisha Graves Otis. Hoists[60] and lifts of various types had been around for years when Otis sprang to fame in the late 1850s. Otis never pretended to have invented the elevator. His contribution was merely to come up with a simple, reliable safety device—a spring mechanism with gripper cogs[61]—that made vertical passenger travel safe. A born showman, Otis traveled the world giving demonstrations of the safety of his elevators. Standing in a heavily weighted elevator, he would have himself hoisted thirty feet or so above the ground, and then call out to an assistant to cut the rope. The audience

---

55 magnate 실력자, 권력자; 거물; an oil magnate 석유왕

56 impracticable 실행 불가능한(unworkable); 쓸 수가 없는(Unusable)

57 preclude 제외하다, 미리 배제하다

58 curtain wall 칸막이 벽(건물의 무게를 지탱하지 않는)

59 without which drafts would be all but uncontrollable, heightening fire risks and making effective heating and cooling an impossibility 회전문이 없었다면 통제할 수 없을 정도의 높은 화재 위험과 효과적인 냉난방을 불가능하게 하는 것 말고는 설계도가 전부였을 것이다.

60 hoist 끌어올리기, 게양; 감아올리는 기계, 호이스트(hoister), 승강기

61 gripper cog 쥐는(집는) 톱니바퀴

would gasp,[62] but instead of crashing to the ground, the elevator would merely drop an inch or so and stay there. He sold the devices by the hundreds. (In 1911 the *New York Tribune* reported that in the previous two years at least 2,600 people had been injured or killed in elevator accidents.)

—Compiled from *Made in America* (pp. 87-99)

62 gasp (놀라서) 숨이 막히다. I gasped with rage.

Exercise

* Answer the questions.

1. What could be one of the best qualities of a rubber?
   a. semi-conductor b. conductor c. transmitter d. insulator

2. Explain the underlined word in the sentence below: how it is combined, auto+bio+graphy.

   He made more money from his autobiography than he ever did from his invention.

3. Change the underlined into opposite idiom.

   The company had nothing to do with him or his descendants.

* Choose the closest meaning to the underlined.

1. Goodyear hastily secured a patent.
   a. steadily-attained b. regularly-got c. quickly-got d. finally-abandoned

2. Goodyear's process was so easily duplicated that other manufacturers simply stole it.
   a. downloaded b. uploaded c. manufactured d. copied

3. With incredible speed, electric lighting became a wonder of the age.
   a. unbelievable b. creditable c. credible d. creative

15-3.

Travel

Most authorities[1] agree that the first real, working car was one devised by the German engineer Gottlieb Daimler in 1884. He call it a *Mercedes*, after his daughter. Unaware of Daimler's creation, another German, Karl Benz, invented a second and very similar car at almost the same time. By this time, however, the concept of an automobile had already been patented in America.

Automobile, a French word concocted[2] from Greek and Latin elements, was at first used only as an adjective, not only to describe cars ("an automobile carriage") but also other self-propelled devices ("automobile torpedo[3]"). By 1899 the word had grown into a noun and was quickly becoming the established general term for cars—though not without opposition. The *New York Times* sniffed[4] that *automobile*, "being half Greek and half Latin, is so near indecent that we print it with hesitation."[5] Before the year was out, the

---

1 authorities 소식통; 권위자
2 concoct 조합하다
3 torpedo 어뢰
4 sniffed 비웃는 투로 말하다
5 Kenneth T. Jackson, *Crabgrass Frontier: The Suburbanization of the United States*, New York: Oxford UP, 1985, Bryson p. 158에서 재인용.

word was being shortened to *auto*. *Car*, from the Latin *carrus* ("two-wheeled wagon"), was first applied to the automobile in 1896, though it had existed in English as a term for various types of wagons since the sixteenth century. By 1910 it had more or less caught up *automobile* in popularity.

Although the early technological developments were almost exclusively German, it was the French who became the first big manufacturers of cars and thus gave us many of the words associated with motoring—*chassis,*[6] *garage, chauffeur, carburetor, coupé,*[7] *limousine*, and of course *automobile* itself.

No big technology in history has taken off more swiftly, more breathtakingly, than the car. And nowhere did it take off faster than in America. In 1898, there were not thirty working cars in the whole of the United States. Within a little over a decade there were not just seven hundred cars in America, but seven hundred car factories. In just the first four months of 1899, American investors provided no less than $388 million of start-up capital for new automobile companies.

They came from every walk of life. John F. and Horace E. Dodge had run a Detroit machine shop. David D. Buick made plumbing supplies. A striking number of the first manufacturers were from the Midwest and particularly from Michigan—Ransom Olds, creator of the Oldsmobile, from Lansing; David D. Buick and Henry Ford from Detroit; William C. Durant, founder of General Motors, from Flint—which helps to explain why Detroit became the Motor City.

---

6 *chassis*[ʃǽsi] (자동차의) 차대, 섀시

7 *coupé* 쿠페형 자동차(sedan보다 작은 2~5인승 자동차)

Exercise

* Read the following passage and answer the questions.

The study of mathematics began in ancient Greece thousands of years ago. It has influenced every branch of scientific discovery through the centuries. The Greeks developed arithmetic for keeping business records. They developed geometry for the study of the sun, stars, and moon. These ancient people delighted in playing games with mathematics. From these games and with their knowledge of arithmetic and geometry, they developed algebra and trigonometry. Over a period of nearly two thousand years mathematics did not change. The ancient thoughts and discoveries were preserved in scattered centers of learning or universities during the Dark Ages. In the 17th century Isaac Newton[8] and Wilhelm Leibnitz[9] invented calculus. But only Newton put this knowledge to practical use. Galileo combined mathematics with physics, also in the 17th century, and thereby linked the two sciences. The 17th century was a time of great mathematical interest and development. Many of our 20th century methods and machines use those 300-year-old theories and methods. The student today learns from centuries of thought and development.

1. When did the study of mathematics begin?

2. Who first developed mathematics?

---

8 Sir Isaac Newton (1642–1726/7) was an English physicist and mathematician (described in his own day as a "natural philosopher") who is widely recognised as one of the most influential scientists of all time and as a key figure in the scientific revolution. His book *Philosophiæ Naturalis Principia Mathematica* ("Mathematical Principles of Natural Philosophy"), first published in 1687, laid the foundations for classical mechanics. Newton also made seminal contributions to optics and shares credit with Gottfried Leibniz for the development of calculus.

9 Gottfried Wilhelm von Leibniz (1646–1716) was a German mathematician and philosopher. He occupies a prominent place in the history of mathematics and the history of philosophy.

3. During which period did mathematics remain unchanged?

4. Who linked the sciences of mathematics and physics?

5. Identify the following names of sciences: politics, economics, ethics, theology, archeology, physiology

* Fill in the blanks with the suitable word(s).

1. Please do a favor _____ me.
   a. by   b. to   c. in   d. for

2. I found the story _________.
   a. incredible   b. physical   c. accidental   d. crashing

3. Morse was widely regarded ____ the greatest man of his age.
   a. into   b. as   c. upon   d. for

* In each of the following sections, fill in the blanks with the correct form—noun, verb, adjective, or adverb. Choose from the words above each section.

〈argument, argue, argumentative〉

1. We had a terrible _________ last night about the dishes.

2. My sister always __________s with me about TV.

3. I think she is an __________ person.

⟨typical, typically⟩

4. __________, my father did crossword puzzle in the evening.

5. A __________ American family watches a lot of TV.

⟨breeze, breezy⟩

6. There was usually a cool ________ on the porch.

7. I liked to sit outside on a ________ evening.

⟨disappear, disappearance⟩

8. When my mother brought out strawberries and cream, they used to __________ very quickly.

9. She was always happy about their __________.

Unit 16

16-1. *Meeting the Perfect Mate*

16-2. *Jonathan and David*

16-3. *Baucis and Philemon*

16-1.

Meeting the Perfect Mate

For the past month I've been taking a graduate seminar called "Social Structure." It's a very popular course. We've been discussing friendship, marriage, and other relationships. One of our assignments is to examine the ways that people meet potential husbands and wives. I've been interviewing students on campus all week as part of my study.

First, I talked with my roommate in the dormitory, Una, a student from Korea.

"What's one way to meet a possible mate?" I asked her.

"Well," she said, "one method in my country is to have a matched marriage."[1]

"A what?" I asked. "I know you can match a tie to a shirt—or two socks after you do the laundry. But people?"

"Sure," she replied. "There aren't many arranged marriages these days, but there were a lot not too long ago. My parents, for example, met each other for the first time on their wedding day. My grandparents chose their children's

1 a matched marriage 중매결혼 cf. matchmaker 중매쟁이

mates and arranged the wedding."

"Do you mean that they weren't in love? That sounds awful! Weren't they upset?"

"Maybe a little bit," Una said, "but they accepted each other. Then, fortunately, they grew to love each other. They've had a good, successful marriage for the past thirty years. This happens in a lot of arranged marriages."

I shook my head. "Amazing!" I said.

The next person that I interviewed was Bill, a guy in my business management class.

"I meet a lot of women in dancing places—at least more than I do on campus," he said. "The environment is interesting and I go every weekend, if possible, to dance or talk or just listen to music."

"That seems great," I said.

"I thought so, too, at first," he said a little sadly. "But on the other hand, very often the women in those places are unfriendly. A lot of men are too aggressive, and the women as a result are very cold."

"Dancing places? Never!" said Julie, a student who works part-time in the campus bookstore. "I prefer to make new friends at places where people have interests in common. I met my boyfriend at the health club, for example, and it seems that the healthy atmosphere of the gym is continuing into the relationship that I have with him."

"That sounds wonderful," I said.

"Yes," she said, "I guess so. But to be honest, there's one problem with this arrangement."

"What?" I asked.

"The truth is that I really hate to exercise, so I don't want to go to the gym anymore. What's my boyfriend going to think when he finds this out?"

"Computer dating services are the answer! said my friend Sara, who lives down the hall from me in the dormitory. "They provide a great way to meet people! The advantage is that you have a lot in common with the people you meet through a computer. The computer can match you up with someone of your same intelligence, astrological sign, age, lifestyle, and personality. For instance, you can meet someone who is creative, competitive, and honest, and you can ask for a scientist, an actor, a vegetarian, or ..."

"Have you had many successful dates so far?" I asked.

"To tell the truth," she said, "no. I think I made a big mistake when I filled out the application form. I didn't want to miss a wonderful guy because of an answer that was too specific, so I was careful to write very general answers."

"What do you mean?"

"Well, there was a question about height. I said 'anyone between 3' 5" (three feet five inches, about 1m 4cm) and 7' 5" (about 2m 25cm).' Then there was a question about recreation. I answered 'yes' to forty-seven interests, from gourmet[2] cooking to camping in the wilderness. I wrote that I liked swimming, hiking, the arts, comedy movies, quiz shows, mystery stories, business, ethnic foods,[3] and so on, but I think that the computer got confused. It hasn't found a date for me since I sent in the application."

Last, I interviewed a guy in the cafeteria.

"Supermarkets," he told me.

"You're kidding," I said.

---

2 gourmet[guərmei] (F) 미식가

3 ethnic foods 외국음식 ethnic 민족의, 이국의

"No, I'm serious. I meet a lot of potential dates over the frozen pizzas in the convenience-food section. Also, it's easy to make small talk over the tomatoes and lettuce in the produce section. We discuss chemicals and nutrition and food prices. Sometimes this leads to a very romantic date."

I slowly shook my head: it is strange ... very strange. I bit my lip because I didn't want to be impolite.

That evening, I talked with my roommate, Una.

"You know," I said. "I think maybe your parents and grand parents had a pretty good idea. A matched marriage is beginning to seem more and more practical to me."

Exercise

* Some words refer to ideas that came before them in the reading.

ex) "My friends have had a good marriage for the past thirty years. This happens in a lot of arranged marriages." (What does *this* refer to? Having a good marriage.)

A. In each of the following sentences, mark the words that the underlined word refers to.

1. I've been taking a graduate seminar in Social Structure for the past month. It's a very popular course.

2. "One method is to have a matched marriage," Una said. "A what?" I asked.

3. "My grandparents chose their children's mates and arranged the wedding," she explained.
   "Do you mean they weren't in love?"

4. "I meet a lot of women in dancing places—at least more than I do on campus.

5. "Dancing places seem great," I said.
   "I thought so at first, too," he said a little sadly.

6. "It seems that the healthy atmosphere in the gym is continuing into our relationship," she said.

"That sounds wonderful," I said.
"Yes," she said, "I guess so."

B. Match each word on the left with its meaning. Write the correct letter on the line.

1. ___ specific	a. boy or man
2. ___ cold	b. not serious
3. ___ height	c. write (in a form)
4. ___ miss	d. the opposite of "general"
5. ___ fill out	e. fruit and vegetables
6. ___ potential	f. how tall a person or thing is
7. ___ guy	g. possible
8. ___ produce	h. unfriendly
9. ___ kidding	i. not find

16-2.

Jonathan and David

Sometime the duties of friendship compete with other obligations and affections. The story of Jonathan, told in the first book of Samuel in the Bible, is one such instance. Jonathan was the eldest son and heir of King Saul of Israel. He was also David's sworn friend. After David killed Goliath, Saul grew jealous of his popularity, and fearing that he would eventually become king, sought to murder him. Jonathan's defense of David, made doubly painful because of his filial duties and his own claim to the throne, is one of our greatest examples of loyalty in friendship.

After David had slain the giant he was brought before King Saul, still holding the giant's head. Saul did not remember in this bold fighting man the boy who a few years before had played in his presence. He took him into his own house, and made him an officer among his soldiers. David was as wise and as brave in the army as he had been when facing the giant, and very soon he was in command of a thousand men. All the men loved him, both in Saul's court and in his camp, for David had the spirit that drew all hearts toward him.

When David was returning from his battle with the Philistines, the women of Israel came to meet him out of the cities, with instruments of music, singing and dancing, and they sang:

"Saul has slain his thousands,
And David has ten thousands."

This made Saul very angry, for he was jealous and suspicious in his spirit. He thought constantly of Samuel's words, that God would take the kingdom from him and would give it to one who was more worthy of it. He began to think that perhaps this young man, who had come in a single day to greatness before the people, might try to make himself king.

His former feeling of unhappiness again came over Saul. He raved[1] in his house, talking as a man talks who is crazed. By this time they all knew that David was a musician, and they called him again to play on his harp and to sing before the troubled king. But now, in his madness, Saul would not listen to David's voice. Twice he threw his spear at him; but each time David leaped aside, and the spear went into the wall of the house.

Saul was afraid of David, for he saw that the Lord was with David, as the Lord was no longer with himself. He would have killed David, but did not dare kill him, because everybody loved David. Saul said to himself, "Though I cannot kill him myself, I will have him killed by the Philistines."

And he sent David out on dangerous errands of war; but David came home in safety, all the greater and the more beloved after each victory. Saul said, "I will give you my daughter Merab for your wife if you will fight the

---

1 rave 소리치다, 고함치다 shout

Philistine for me."

David fought the Philistines; but when he came home from the war he found that Merab, who had been promised to him, had been given as wife to another man. Saul had another daughter, named Michal. She loved David, and showed her love for him. Then Saul sent word to David, saying, "You shall have Michal, my daughter, for your wife when you have killed a hundred Philistines."

Then David went out and fought the Philistines, and killed two hundred of them; and they brought the word to Saul. Then Saul gave him his daughter Michal as his wife; but he was all the more afraid of David as he saw him growing in power and drawing nearer to the throne of the kingdom.

But if Saul hated David, Saul's son Jonathan saw David's courage, and the soul of Jonathan was knit to the soul of David, and Jonathan loved him as his own soul. He took off his own royal robe, and his sword, and his bow, and gave them all to David. It grieved[2] Jonathan greatly that his father, Saul, was so jealous of David. He spoke to his father, and said: "Let not the king do harm to David; for David has been faithful to the king, and he has done great things for the kingdom. He took his life in his hand, and killed the Philistine, and won a great victory for the Lord and for the people. Why should you seek to kill an innocent man?"

For the time Saul listened to Jonathan, and said, "As the Lord lives, David shall not be put to death."

And again David sat at the king's table, among the princes; and when Saul was troubled again David played on his harp and sang before him. But once more Saul's jealous anger arose, and he threw his spear at David. David

2 grieve 슬프게 하다 (n) grief

was watchful and quick. He leaped aside, and, as before, the spear fastened into the wall.

Saul sent men to David's house to seize him; but Michal, Saul's daughter, who was David's wife, let David down out of the window, so that he escaped. She placed an image on David's bed and covered it with the bedclothes. When the men came, she said, "David is ill in the bed, and cannot go."

They brought the word to Saul, and he said, "Bring him to me in the bed, just as he is."

When the image was found in David's bed, David was in a safe place, far away. David went to Samuel at Ramah, and stayed with him among the men who were prophets worshipping God and singing and speaking God's word. Saul heard that David was there, and sent men to take him. But when these men came and saw Samuel and the prophets praising God and praying, the same spirit came on them, and they began to praise and to pray. Saul sent other men, but these also, when they came among the prophets, felt the same power, and joined in the worship.

Finally, Saul said, "If no other man will bring David to me, I will go myself and take him."

And Saul went to Ramah; but when he came near to the company of the worshippers, praising God, and praying, and preaching, the same spirit came on Saul. He, too, began to join in the songs and the prayers, and stayed there all that day and that night, worshipping God very earnestly. When the next day he went again to his home in Gibeah, his feeling was changed for the time, and he was again friendly to David.

But David knew that Saul was at heart his bitter enemy and would kill kim if he could as soon as his madness came upon him. He met Jonathan out in the field away from the place. Jonathan said to David:

"Stay away from the king's table for a few days, and I will find out how he feels toward you, and will tell you. Perhaps even now my father may become your friend. But if he is to be your enemy, I know that the Lord is with you, and that Saul will not succeed against you. Promise me that as long as you live you will be kind to me, and not only to me while I live, but to my children after me."

Jonathan believed, as many others believed, that David would yet[3] become the king of Israel, and he was willing to give up to David his right to be king, such was his great love for him. That day a promise was made between Jonathan and David, that they and their children, and those who should come after them, should be friends forever.

Jonathan said to David, "I will find how my father feels toward you, and will bring you word. After three days I will be here with my bow and arrows, and I will send a little boy out near your place of hiding, and I will shoot three arrows. If I say to the boy, 'Run, find the arrows, they are on this side of you,' then you can come safely, for the king will not harm you. But if I call out to the boy, 'The arrows are away beyond you,' that will mean that there is danger, and you must hide from the king."

So David stayed away from Saul's table for two days. At first Saul said nothing of his absence, but at last he said:

"Why has not the son of Jesse come to meals yesterday and today?"

And Jonathan said, "David asked leave of me to go to his home at Bethlehem and visit his oldest brother."

Then Saul was very angry. He cried out, "You are a disobedient son! Why

3 yet 언젠가는, 머지않아, 조만간

have you chosen this enemy of mine as your best friend? Do you not know that as long as he is alive you can never be king? Send after him, and let him be brought to me, for he shall surely die!"

Saul was so fierce in his anger that he threw his spear at his own son Jonathan. Jonathan rose up from the table, so anxious for his friend David that he could eat nothing. The next day, at the hour agreed upon, Jonathan went out into the field with a little boy. He said to the boy, "Run out yonder, and be ready to find the arrows that I shoot."

And as the boy was running Jonathan shot arrows beyond him, and he called out, "The arrows are away beyond you; run quickly and find them."

The boy ran and found the arrows, and brought them to Jonathan. He gave the bow and arrows to the boy, saying to him, "Take them back to the city. I will stay here awhile."

And as soon as the boy was out of sight David came from his hiding place and ran to Jonathan. They fell into each other's arms and kissed each other again and again, and wept together. For David knew now that he must no longer hope to be safe in Saul's hands. He must leave home, and wife, and friends, and his father's house, and hide wherever he could from the hate of King Saul.

Jonathan said to him, "Go in peace; for we have sworn together saying, 'The Lord shall be between you and me, and between your children and my children forever.'"

Then Jonathan went again to his father's palace, and David went out to find a hiding place.

—From *The Book of Virtues* (pp. 299–303)

Exercise

* Choose the closest meaning to the underlined.

1. Jonathan was willing to <u>give up</u> to David his right to be king.
   a. yield   b. declare   c. promise   d. claim

2. Saul sent men to David's house to <u>seize</u> him.
   a. loose   b. take   c. detect   d. chase

* Translate the following proverbs into Korean.

1. Do not protect yourself by a fence, but rather by friends.

2. Out of sight, out of mind.

3. Prosperity makes friends, adversity tries them.

4. Lend your money and lose your friend.

5. Birds of a feather flock together.

6. A man is known by the company he keeps.

7. A friend in need is a friend indeed.

16-3.

Baucis and Philemon

The ancient Greeks understood that the health of the community depended on how well its individual citizens treated one another. To them, Zeus, the king of the gods, was both the guardian of the state and the protector of human relations among civilized men. All social institutions, including the family, lay in his care. Travelers in particular honored him, for he rewarded those who remembered the rules of hospitality and duties of friendship, as we see in this story in which Zeus and Hermes (Jupiter and Mercury to the Romans) seek shelter among the mortals.

Once upon a time Jupiter, in human shape, visited the land of Phrygia, and with him Mercury, without his wings. They presented themselves as weary travelers at many a door, seeking rest and shelter, but found all closed; for it was late, and the inhospitable inhabitants would not rouse[1] themselves to open for their reception. At last a small thatched cottage received them, where Baucis, a pious old dame, and her husband, Philemon, had grown old together. Not ashamed of their poverty, they made it endurable by moderate desires and

1 rouse[rauz] 깨우다, 일으키다

kind dispositions. When the two guests crossed the humble threshold and bowed their heads to pass under the low door, the old man placed a seat, on which Baucis, bustling and attentive, spread a cloth, and begged them to sit down. Then she raked out the coals from the ashes, kindled a fire, and prepared some pot-herbs and bacon for them. A beechen[2] bowl was filled with warm water, that their guests might wash. While all was doing, they beguiled[3] the time with conversation.

The old woman with trembling hand set the table. One leg was shorter than the rest, but a piece of slate put under restored the level. When it was steady, she rubbed the table down with sweet-smelling herbs. Upon it she set some of chaste[4] Minerva's olives, some cornel berries preserved in vinegar,[5] and added radishes and cheese, with egg lightly cooked in the ashes. The meal was served in earthen dishes; and an earthenware pitcher, with wooden cups, stood beside them. When all was ready the stew, smoking hot, was set on the table. Some wine, not of the oldest, was added, and for dessert, apples and wild honey.

Now while the repast[6] proceeded, the old folks were astonished to see that the wine, as fast as it was poured out, renew itself in the pitcher of its own accord.[7] Struck with terror, Baucis and Philemon recognized their heavenly guests, fell on their knees, and with clasped hands implored forgiveness for their poor entertainment. There was an old goose, which they kept as the guardian of their humble cottage, and they bethought them to make this a sacrifice in

2 beechen[biːtʃən] 너도밤나무의
3 beguiled 즐겁게 보내다
4 chaste 순결한
5 some cornel berries preserved in vinegar 식초에 절인 약간의 산딸기
6 repast: meal
7 of its own accord 저절로

honor of their guests. But the goose, too nimble[8] for the old folk, with the aid of feet and wings eluded[9] their pursuit and at last took shelter between the gods themselves. They forbade it to be slain, and spoke in these words: "We are gods. This inhospitable village shall pay the penalty of its impiety; you alone shall go free from the chastisement.[10] Quit your house and come with us to the top of yonder hill." They hastened to obey. The country behind them was speedily sunk in a lake, only their own house left standing. While they gazed with wonder at the sight, that old house of theirs was changed. Columns took the place of the corner posts, the thatch grew yellow and appeared a gilded roof, the floors became marble, the doors were enriched with carving and ornaments of gold. Then spoke Jupiter in benign[11] accents: "Excellent old man, and woman worthy of such a husband, speak, tell us your wishes. What favor have you to ask of us?" Philemon took counsel with Baucis a few moments, then declared to the gods their common wish. "We ask to be priests and guardians of this thy temple, and that one and the same hour may take us both from life." Their prayer was granted. When they had attained a great age, as they stood one day before the steps of the sacred edifice and were telling the story of the place, Baucis saw Philemon begin to put forth leaves, and Philemon saw Baucis changing in like manner. While still they exchanged parting words, a leafy crown grew over their heads. "Farewell, dear spouse," they said together, and at the same moment the bark closed over their mouths. The Tyanean shepherd still shows the two trees—an oak and a linden,[12] standing side by side.

—From *The Book of Virtues* (pp. 303-304)

8 nimble 재빠른, 민첩한
9 elude 피하다
10 chastisement[tʃæstáizmənt] 응징
11 benign 자비로운, 다정한
12 linden 린덴(참피나무)

Exercise

* Choose the closest meaning to the underlined.

1. An architect builds imposing edifices.

   a. stadiums b. structures c. temples d. columns

2. Zeus was both the guardian of the state and the protector of human relations among civilized men.

   a. matron b. prophet c. protector d. founder

3. They presented themselves as weary travelers at many a door.

   a. upset b. careful c. mortal d. tired

4. The inhospitable inhabitants would not rouse themselves to open for their reception.

   a. unkind b. careless c. poor d. endurable

5. Not ashamed of their poverty, they made it endurable by moderate desires and kind dispositions.

   a. generous, characteristics b. temperate, inclinations

   c. patient, features d. huge, traits

6. When the two guests crossed the humble threshold and bowed their heads to pass under the low door, the old man placed a seat, on which Baucis, bustling and attentive, spread a cloth, and begged them to sit down.

   a. luxurious–careless b. costly–seeking

   c. broken–shameful d. poor–careful

7. The old folks were <u>astonished</u> to see the wine.

a. surprised　b. embarrassed　c. scared　d. relieved

8. This inhospitable village shall pay the <u>penalty</u> of its impiety.

a. sacrifice　b. punishment　c. amount　d. token

* Choose the opposite meaning to the underlined.

1. He rewarded those who remembered the rules of <u>hospitality</u> and duties of friendship.

a. hospital　b. hospitalization　c. hostility　d. habit

2. Zeus and Hermes seek shelter among the <u>mortals</u>.

a. immortals　b. humans　c. cottages　d. buildings

부 록

1. 수 접두어(그리스어 및 라틴어)
2. 리포트 작성
3. 바꾸어 말하기(Paraphrasing)
4. Vocabulary Building

1. 수 접두어(그리스어 및 라틴어)

Number	Greek	Latin
0	a–/an– (another)	in– (intangible)
$\frac{1}{2}$	hemi– (hemisphere)	semi–/demi– (semicolon, demigod)
1	mono– (monologue, monotonous)	uni–
2	di– (dialogue, diverge)	duo–/bi– (duo, bilingual)
3	tri– (triple)	tre–/ter– (tertiary)
4	tetra–/tetr–	quadri–/quadr–
9	ennea–	nona–/non–
10	deka–/deca	deci–
어떤 수(Any no.) 〉 1	poly–	multi–

2. 리포트 작성

기본적으로 문자의 위계질서를 따른다. 예를 들어 논문이나 보고서 제목은 진한 고딕체 16포인트로 하고 본문 내의 소제목은 신명조체 12포인트를 사용하며, 본문에는 10포인트 크기의 바탕체를 사용하는 등의 관례를 따른다. 필요에 따라 본문 텍스트 내에서도 글자를 진하게 하거나 기울이거나 글자에 밑줄을 긋기도 한다.

3. 바꾸어 말하기(Paraphrasing)

To understand and remember information in a reading, it often helps to "paraphrase" it—that is, to say it another way.

ex) Two recent changes are making modern medicine a more popular and exciting field of study than ever before.

* For each of the following items, circle the letter of the paraphrase(the sentence with a similar meaning).

1. Fortunately, new technology is now available to modern "disease detectives" who are putting together clues to solve medical mysteries.

a. Modern science helps "disease detectives" answer the questions of medicine.
b. We are fortunate to have technology in medicine.
c. Detectives need new clues to solve the mysteries of sick people.

2. Transplants of the heart, liver, kidney, and other organs of the body are much more common than they were ten or twenty years ago.
   a. Transplants of body organs were not common ten years ago.
   b. The heart, the liver, and the kidney are organs; doctors transplant them from one body to another much more often now than previously.
   c. People with organ transplants are much healthier than people who lived twenty years ago.

3. Because of modern technology, organ transplants are more successful today than they were in the past. Not long ago, transplant patients often died after a few days because their bodies fought against the new organ. A new drug, however, now helps the human body accept its new part.
   a. Organ transplants were not successful in the past because doctors did not give their patients drugs.
   b. Today, patients never die after an organ transplant because their bodies accept it.
   c. With a new drug, organ transplants succeed mor often because the patient's body not fight against the new organ.

4. Vocabulary Building

* Roots: a root is the basic element－fundamental or essential part－of a word.

Root	Meaning and Example
ag, act	do, act; as agent, counteract
agr	field; agriculture
alt	high; altitude, altar
alter	other; alternative
am	friend, love; amenity, amorous
anim	feeling, sprit; unanimous, animosity
ann	year; annual
anthrop	man; philanthropy,
aper	open; aperture
apt	fit; adapt, aptitude
aqu	water; aquarium
arch	rule, govern; anarchy
aster, astr	star; disaster, astronomy
aud	hear; audition
aur	gold; auriferous (금을 함유한)
bas	low; debase, basement
bell	war; bellicose
ben	good, well; benevolent
bibl	book; biblical, bibliography
bio	life; biology
brev	short; brevity, abbreviation
cad, cas, cid	fall; casualty, incident
cand	white, shining; candid, candidate
cap, capt	take, hold; capable, captive
capit	head; capital
carn	flesh; carnal, carnivorous
ced, cess	yield, go; procession
celer	swift; accelerate
cent	hundred; century

chrom	color; chromatic (색채의, 채색한)
chron	time; chronology
cid, cis	cut, kill; suicide, precision
clin	lean, bend; inclination, recline
clud, clus	close, shut; conclude
cogn	know; recognize
cord	heart; accord
corp	body; corpse
cosm	world; cosmic, cosmopolitan
cred	believe; incredible
curr, curs	run; current
dec	ten; decade
dem	people; democracy
derm	skin; dermatologist
di	day; diary
dic, dict	speak, say; indicate, contradict
dign	worthy; dignity
domin	lord, master; dominate
dorm	sleep; dormitory
duc, duct	lead; induce
ego	I; egotism
equ	equal; equity
fac, fact, fect, fic	make, do; factory, infection, fiction
fer	bear, carry; fertile, confer
fid	faith, trust; infidelity
fin	end; infinite, final
flect, flex	bend; reflect, flexible
form	shape; conform, reformation
fort	strong; fortitude
frag, fract	break; fragile, fracture
fug	flee; fugitive, refugee
fus	pour; confuse, fusion
gen	kind, race, birth; generate, genration

gest	carry, bring; congestion
grad, gress	step, go; graduate
graph	write; autograph, graphic
grat	pleasing; gratitude, congratulate
hydr	water; dehydrated
integr	entire, whole; integrate
ject	throw; inject, projection
junct	join; juncture
lat	carry; translation
leg, lig, lect	choose, gather; eligible, collect
liber	free; liberate
loc	place; local
log	word, study; psychology
magn	great; magnitude, magnificent
man	hand; manufacture, manual
mar	sea; marine
mater	mother; maternal, matrimony
mega	large; megaton, megaphone
ment	mind; mentality
merg	plunge, sink; submerge, merger
meter	measure; symmetry
migr	wander; migrate, immigration
mir	look; admire, mirror
mit, miss	send; admit, submission
mon	advise, remind; admonish, monument
mort	death; immortality, mortal
mot, mov	move; motor, movable
mult	many; multitude
mut	change; mutation, immutable
nat	born; innate
nav	ship; naval, navigate
neg	deny; negate
nomen	name; nominee

nov	new; novelty, innovation
oper	work; cooperation, operate
pater, patri	father; paternal, patriot
ped, pod	foot; biped, triped
ped	child; pedagogue
pel, puls	drive; compel, expulsion
pend, pens	hang; pendant, pension
pet	seek; impetus, petition
phil	loving; philosophy
phon	sound; phone, phonetics
plic	fold, bend; complicate
pon, pos	place, put; component, compose
poten	powerful; potential
psych	mind; psychological
que(i)r, qui(e)s	ask, seek; inquiry, quest
re(i)g, rect	rule, govern; rigid, corrective
rid, ris	laugh; ridiculous
rupt	break; erupt, interruption
sacr, sanct	holy; sacrifice, sacred, sanctify
sci, scio	know; science, conscious
scop	watch; telescope
scrib, script	write; describe, prescription
sec, sect	cut; bisect
sent, sens	feel, think; sentiment, sensible
serv	keep; reserve, conservation
sist	place, stand; assist, resistance
soph	wisdom; sophisticated, philosophy
spec, spect, spic	look, appear; prospect, conspicuous
spir	breathe; respiration
stat, stab	stand; status, stability
stru, struct	build; construct, destructive
sum, sumpt	take; assume, presumption
tele	distance; telephone

tempor	time; temporary
ten, tain	hold; reach; tenant, retain
term	end; terminal, terminate
ter, terr	land, earth; terrace
therm	heat; thermometer
tract	draw; attract
umbra	shade; umbrella
urb	city; suburb, urban
vac	empty; evacuation
val, vail	be strong; valid, prevail
vert, vers	turn; convert, reverse
vid, vis	see; evident, visible
viv, vit	live; survive, vital
volv, volut	roll, turn; involve, revolution

Prefix	Meaning and Example
a, ab, abs	from, away; absent
ad	to; adhere
ante, anti	before; anticipate
anti	against; antislavery
arch	first, chief; archangel
auto	self; autobiography, automatic
ben	good, well; benefactor
bi	two; binocular
circum	around; circumstance
com, con, col, cor, co	together; company, conversation, collect, correct, co-worker
contra, contro, counter	against; contradict, counteract
de	down, away from, about; descend, depart, describe
demi	half; demigod
dia	across, through; diameter
dis, di, dif	apart, not; division
ex, e, ef	out of, from; extract, eject, efface

extra	out of, beyond; extraordinary
hyper	too much; hypersensitive
in, il, im, ir	into, in, on; invade, illustrate, immerse, irritate
in, il, im, ir	not; indistinct, illegal, impossible, irresponsible
inter, intro	between, among; international, introduce
mal	bad; maltreat, malevolent
mono	one, single; monotonous
neo	new; neophyte
non	not; nonconformist
ob, of, op	against; offend, oppose
omni	all; omniscient, omnipresent
ortho	straight; orthodox
pan	all; pantheism
peri	around; perimeter
poly	many; polygamy
post	after; postpone
pro	forward, before; proceed, provide
re	back, again; recollection, recede
retro	backwards; retrospect
se	apart, away; separate
semi	half; semicircle
sub	under; submarine
super	above, beyond; supernatural
syn, sym	with, at the same time; synonym, sympathy
trans	across; transmit
ultra	beyond; ultramodern
un	not; unaware, uninformed
uni	one; uniform
vice	instead of; vice-president

Suffix	Meaning and Example
acious, cious	having the quality of; capacious
age	act, condition; courage
al	belonging to; legal
ance, ence	state of; abundance, indulgence, presence
ate	one who; candidate, advocate
ary, eer, er	one who, concerning; secretary, engineer, mariner
cy	state, position of; presidency
dom	state of; freedom, kingdom
er, or	one who; player, actor
fy	make; beautify
hood	state of; childhood
ic, id	of, like; bucolic, acrid
il, ile	capable of being; evil
ion	act of; perspiration
ious	characterized by; spacious, illustrious
ish	like; boyish, foolish
ism	belief in or practice of; idealism, capitalism
ist	one who practises or is devoted to; anarchist, harpist
ive	relating to; abusive
mony	state of; harmony, matrimony
ness	quality of; willingness
or, er	one who; monitor, employer
ory	a place for; factory
ous, ose	full of; ponderous
ship	state of, skill; friendship
some	characteristic of; fearsome
tude	state of; rectitude
ward	in the direction of; backward
y	full of; showy

■ 참고문헌

고창석. 『레토릭 영어명언』. 경기도 파주: 한국학술정보, 2013.

Becker, Lawrence. *A History of Western Ethics.* New York: Routledge, 2003.

Bennett, William J. ed. *The Book of Virtues: A Treasury of Great Moral Stories.* New York: Simon & Schuster, 1993.

Bryson, Bill. *Made in America: An Informal History of the English Language in the United States.* New York: William Morrow and Co., Inc., 1994.

Bulfinch, Thomas. *Bulfinch's Mythology: The Age of Fable.* Garden City, NY: Doubleday Book & Music clubs, Inc., 1968.

Clark, William L. *Spoken American English: Advanced Course.* 서울: 외국어이학사, 1978.

Coelho, Paulo. *The Pilgrimage.* trans. Alan Clarke. NY: HarperCollins, 1995.

Communicative English Program. Seoul: Sam Seong Publishing Co., 1976.

Geertz, Clifford. *The Interpretation of Cultures.* London: Hutchinson, 1975.

Gruber, Gary R. *Gruber's Complete Preparation for the SAT.* 5th ed. New York: HarperPerennial, 1992.

Hamilton, Edith. *Mythology.* Boston, Mass: New American Library, 1969.

Jackson, Kenneth T. *Crabgrass Frontier: The Suburbanization of the United States.* New York: Oxford UP, 1985.

Jacobus, Lee A. ed. *Aesthetics and the Arts.* New York: McGraw-Hill, 1968.

Jones, Maldwyn Allen. *American Immigration.* Chicago: U of Chicago P, 1960.

Kirn, Elaine et al. 2nd ed. *Interactions I: A Reading Skills Book.* New York: McGraw-Hill Publishing Co., 1990.

Lee A. Jacobus. ed. *Aesthetics and the Arts.* New York: McGraw-Hill, 1968.

Lee, Peter H. compiled & ed. *Modern Korean Literature: An Anthology.* Honolulu, USA: U of Hawaii P. 262-66.

Mumford, Lewis. *Faith for Living.* from *A University Anthology for Overseas Students.* London: Longmans, 1955. 293-95.

Reading Adventures 2. Boston, MA: National Geographic Learning, 2013.

Schacter, Daniel. *PSYCHOLOGY.* United States of America: Catherine Woods, 2011.

Shweder, Richard A. "Moral Maps, "First World" Conceits, and the New Evangelists." *Culture Matters: How Values Shape Human Progress.* Eds. Lawrence E. Harrison & Samuel P. Huntington. NY: Basic Books, 2000. 158-76.

Stamp, L. Dudley. *"Our Undeveloped World."* from *A University Anthology for Overseas Students.* London: Longmans, 1955. 137-39.

Turvey, John. simplified. *Tales from the Arabian Nights.* Essex, England: Longman, 1989.

Wolfe, Thomas. Cleanth Brooks and Robert Penn Warren. eds. 2nd ed. "The Far and the Near." *Understanding Fiction.* New York: Appleton-Century-Crofts, Inc., 1959. 422-25.

http://www.psychologytoday.com/basics/motivation

http://en.wikipedia.org/wiki

http://www.dailymail.co.uk/news/article-2551059/South-Koreans-drink-TWICE-Russians-five-times-Brits.html

고창석
전남대학교 영어영문학 학사
미국 애리조나 주립대학교 대학원 영문학 석사
성균관대학교 대학원 영어영문학 박사
현재 초당대학교 교수

에이스 English Readings

초판 1쇄 발행일: 2015년 2월 28일
편저자: 고창석
발행인: 이성모
발행처: 도서출판 동인 / 서울시 종로구 혜화로3길 5 118호
등 록: 제1-1599호
TEL: (02) 765-7145 / FAX: (02) 765-7165
E-mail: dongin60@chol.com

ISBN 978-89-5506-653-1
정가 18,000원